The Great American
CONVERTIBLE

BY THE AUTO EDITORS OF CONSUMER GUIDE®

BEEKMAN HOUSE

Louis Weber, C.E.O.
Publications International, Ltd.
7373 North Cicero Avenue
Lincolnwood, Illinois 60646

Permission is never granted for commercial purposes.

Printed and bound in Yugoslavia

8   7   6   5   4   3   2   1

Library of Congress Catalog Card Number: 90-63307

ISBN 0-517-03584-7

This edition published by Beekman House,
distributed by Outlet Book Company, Inc.,
a Random House Company,
225 Park Avenue South, New York, New York 10003

Credits

Special thanks to the owners of the convertibles featured in this book for their enthusiastic cooperation. They are listed below, along with the page number(s) on which their cars appear:

Walter J. Smith—4-5, 150; Phil Kuhn III—6-7; Jim Bowerson—8-9; Terry Radey—10, 11; Owen Hoyt—12,13; Milford "Red" Curtis—15; William E. Stever—17; S. Ray Miller, Jr.—18, 19, 36, 70; Larry Klein—20; Bill Trnka—21; Bob Avery—24; Ben Caskey, Jr.—25; Dr. Barbara Atwood—26; Murray Hall—27; Ed Warner—30; Wayne Graefen—31; Ernest J. Toth, Jr.—33; Gene Perkins—34; Dick Pyle—37; Evan & Dolores Martin—39; Robert Zaitlin—40-41; Harv Sjaarda—42; Leonard Zannini—44; Carol Nesladek—44; G. Kanaan—45; Walter G. Serviss—46; Bruce Kennedy—50, 51; Tom Hall—52, 55, 62; Darvin & Becca Kuehl—53; Neil Torrence—54; Ed Gunther—54; Clay Nichols—56; Armand Annerau—57; Wm. Lyon Collection—58-59; Rod Morris—59; Jerry Emery—60; Jack Passey, Jr.—60; Richard DeFendorf—61; Len Vinegard—61; Ralph Geissler—63, 78; Robert G. Hall—65; Walter Thomas—65; Harry A. Demenge—66-67, 80, 127; J.H. Bowersox—68-69, 188; Leonard Galardi—68; Bill & Berta Honey—72-73; Eugene Tareshawey—73; Terry Johnson—74-75, 78-79; Donald E. Desing—76; John Poochigian—76; Henry & Joan Rehm—77; Harry Wynn—78, 82; Domino's Classic Cars, Ann Arbor, MI—81; Joseph Leir—82-83; Vincent Dahl—84; Suburban Motors, Tucson, AZ—84; Robert N. Carlson—86; Bill Schwanbeck—86; Blaine Jenkins—86, 120, 168-169; Roger O. Kash—87; Jack Bart 88; Thomas F. Lerch—89; Vincent Rufullo—89; William E. Goodsene 90; Charles Beed—90; Burt Van Flue—90; Art Sabin—91; Ken Hutchinson—92; Bob Hill—93; Marshall Burton—93; Eldon T. Anson—94-95; Bill Bost—96; Jerry & Jackie Lew—97; Ken Havekost—98-99; Robert Rocchio—100-101; Chuck Rizzo—103; Bud Manning—107; John Sanders—108-109; Kurt Fredricks—110-111; Larry Wilson—112; Gary Gettleman—112; Tim Graves—114; Stanley & Phyllis Dumes—114; Glen Gangestad—115; John Baker—116; Ramshead Auto Collection—116-117; Richard P. Lesson—118; Paul & Nancy Vlcek—119; Mearl Zeigler—119; Peter & Jane Schlacter—120; Gary Robinson—121; David Studer—122; Billy J. Harris—122; David Burkholder—123; Bob Weber—123; Jim Clark—124, 132; Jackie Tinker—124; Mervin Afflerbach—125, 130-131; Jim Cahill—125; Jeff & Aleta Wells—126; Gary Richards—128-129; Norb Kopchinski—129; Raymond & Marilyn Benoy—130; June Trombley—131; Joe Malta—132; Glen Warrick—132-133; Gary Johns—134; Ross Gibaldi—134; John Krempasky—135, 140; Marvin & Joan Hughes—137; Amos Minter—138-139; Bob Rose—138; Dick Hoyt—141; Michael L. Berzenye—142; Jerry Hammer—143; Tim Fagan—143; Maurice Hawa—143; Dennis L. Huff—144-145; Kris Trexler—146; Mark Apel—146-147; Jerry Cinotti—148-149; Richard Carpenter—151; Sam Harpster—152-153; Frank Ellis—152; George Dalinis—153; Jim Davidson—154-155; Rick Schick—156, 200-201; Thomas J. Patterson—156-157; Terry Lucas—158-159; Bill Hall—159; Charlie Wells—160-161; George Kling—162-163; Jim Heidenway—162; Dave & Norma Wasilewski—163; Dean Stansfield—164; Harold Lee Lockhart—164; Vivan Riley—164; Ray Shinn—165; Paul Garlick—166-167; Roger Randolph—166; Sam Scoles—168; Larry E. Driscoll—170; John L. Gaylord—170; Dean J. Moroni—171; Chuck Henderson—171; Kenneth & Linda Coleman—172-173; Joseph Pessetti—174; Tom West—175; Robert Hallada—175; Dick Tarnutzer, Dells Museum, WI—177; Wanda Habenicht—179; Jackie Peacock—180; Daniel Mitchell—180; Gladys Duzell—181; Mike & Marge Tanzer—181; Joe Kelly—182; Mr. & Mrs. Ralph M. Mathiot—182; Bay Banuls—184; Scott Brubaker—185; Connie Davis—185; Vince & Helen Springer—185; Sherman Williams—186; Austin Fray—186; Richard & Joyce Dollmeyer—188-189; Alice Greunke—190; Denny Allen—191; Sid Slayton—191; Ron Embleton—192-193; Mike & Yvonne Tifft—192; Don & Linda Davis—193; Lou Schultz Jr.—194-195; Jim Ashworth—196; Charley Lillard—197; James E. Collins—197; Randy O'Daniel—198-199; Otis Chandler—202; Leroy Lasiter—202-203; Steve Engeman—203; Joseph Whitey Ererle—205; Jack Karleskind—206; Dale Lingle—206-207; Ed Oberhaus—208-209, 219; Frank Trummer—212-213; Ron Miller—212; Larry Zidek—214-215; Mike Alter—214; Patricia A. Schelli—216; Gilbert & Hollis Bierman—217.

The editors gratefully acknowledge the photographers who helped make this book possible. They are listed below, along with page number(s) of their photos:

Nicky Wright—4-5, 18, 19, 34, 36, 42, 70, 81, 86, 90, 94-95, 112, 122, 144-145, 150, 162-163, 168-169, 175, 180, 185, 186, 198-199, 202-203, 208-209, 212, 217, 219; Bud Juneau—8-9, 12, 13, 17, 20, 50, 51, 54, 57, 60, 63, 68-69, 73, 78, 82, 93, 97, 112, 114-115, 116-117, 121, 131, 146-147, 156-157, 175, 188, 193, 196, 197, 206; Larry Gustin, Buick PR—12, 13, 33, 35, 57, 63, 91, 106, 136, 180, 183, 236; Milton Gene Kieft—10, 11, 14, 16, 33, 45, 61, 86, 89, 104-105, 120, 134, 152-153, 160-161, 185; Helen J. Earley, Oldsmobile History Center, Lansing, MI—43, 49, 53, 66-67, 140, 215; Henry Austin Clark, Jr.—15, 68; Doug Mitchel—21, 26, 37, 44, 53, 56, 61, 65, 71, 76, 77, 78, 84, 86, 87, 88, 89, 91, 93, 96, 102, 105, 107, 108-109, 113, 119, 123, 125, 126, 127, 129, 130, 134, 136, 143, 153, 156, 162, 164, 165, 166, 170, 171, 173, 174, 179, 181, 182, 183, 185, 186, 188-189, 191, 194, 200-201, 210-211, 216, 222, 223; Dan Lyons—24, 88, 90, 116, 118, 124, 132, 164, 182; Vince Manocchi—25, 31, 40-41, 46, 54, 58-59, 60, 66-67, 76, 80, 82-83, 87, 100-101, 123, 127, 128-129, 129, 132, 136, 141, 142, 143, 148-149, 149, 151, 154-155, 158-159, 159, 168, 178, 180, 190, 214; Richard Spiegelman—26, 27, 49; Chuck Ordowski, Ford Photographic—37, 83, 87, 93, 106, 135, 195, 197, 204, 213; Ed Goldberger—39, 84, 90; Chrysler Historical Collection—43, 77, 85, 92, 126, 136, 145, 161, 167, 172, 174, 177; Sam Griffith—44, 52, 55, 62, 92, 110-111, 115, 123, 124, 164, 179, 181, 192-193, 194-195, 204, 214-215, 233, 240-241, 245; Mike Mueller—59, 72-73, 114, 137, 172-173, 197; Kari St. Antoine, Chev. PR—69, 85, 176, 209, 228-229, 234, 235, 238-239, 240, 242, 246, 247; Jim Thompson—74-75, 78-79, 203; Thomas Glatch—103, 122, 135, 140, 177, 212-213; Joe Bohovic—125, 130-131, 192, 205; Jerry Heasley—132-133, 202; Bob Tenney—138-139; Kris Trexler—146; S. Scott Hutchinson—166-167; Chrylser PR—220-221, 224, 225, 226, 229, 237, 247, 248; Sheila Main, Pontiac PR—223, 230, 234, 248; Chris Wallace, Cadillac PR—224, 232, 234, 246; Dodge PR—225, 226, 228, 247; Patty A. Schuetz, Excalibur PR—227; Frank Peiler—234; Larry Weis, Ford PR—236, 242-243, 248; Ross Ruehle, Oldsmobile PR—237, 244-245, 248.

TABLE OF CONTENTS

INTRODUCTION

*C*onvertibles have long symbolized the romantic side of motoring. While they initially offered a degree of practicality as a convenient provider of both warm and cold weather comfort, style was always the top priority. Somehow, drivers behind the wheel of a convertible seemed to enjoy an inner exuberance best left for poets to describe.

Though their practicality today is questionable at best, convertibles are rarely purchased for their pragmatic appeal. The advent of effective air conditioning systems rendered ragtops obsolete as a hedge against hot weather, making their vices all the more apparent. While this undoubtedly contributed to their temporary demise in the late Seventies, convertibles are back with us today solely on the strength of their charisma. Few bother calling them sensible; their appeal is to more basic human emotions.

Throughout their history, convertibles have barely made a dent in overall year-to-year production figures. Though some convertible numbers may seem rather substantial (sales peaked at over 500,000 units in 1965), ragtops rarely garnered more than a five percent share of the market. That they've lived and prospered as long as they have is probably due more to their allure and prestige value than to their actual sales. Convertibles represent the *ne plus ultra* of cars as we know them—stars that illuminate the maker's entire model line. Though the customer's check may be made out for a station wagon, it was often the drop-top that drew the buyer into the showroom.

To their owners, however, any objections are overshadowed by the emotionally powerful fact that convertibles are simply more fun to drive than other cars. Never mind that for about 300 days a year their toys cannot be enjoyed to the fullest unless they happen to live in the sun belt—or are slightly masochistic.

There's no mystery about the convertible's history, nor are its origins difficult to pinpoint. It all started in the late Twenties, when automotive body engineers contrived to make the roadster and touring car, then the dominant open body types, into something a bit more civilized by giving them folding tops and roll-up windows.

Nevertheless, we ought to be clear about how car people define a convertible as opposed to other open styles like roadsters, runabouts, and phaetons. There's not much argument: A convertible must have a top that is permanently attached to a framework that you fold down—either by hand or with power assist—rather than remove completely (as you do the top of an MG sports car, for instance). Stricter enthusiasts add that a convertible must have roll-up windows as well: The winsome Dodge Wayfarer was considered a "roadster" in

1949 (when it had side curtains), a convertible in 1950 (when its windows rolled up).

Of course, a convertible may have either two or four doors. As a two-door it was first referred to as a "cabriolet," later a "convertible coupe." Four-door styles have gone by many different names over the years, but most have been termed "convertible sedans."

Manufacturers haven't helped latterday chroniclers, however. GM called its convertible sedans "convertible phaetons," which wasn't really accurate (a true phaeton seats five or more passengers and has a take-off top). Hudson for many years called its convertible coupes "broughams," which to the rest of the industry meant two-door sedan. Chrysler had a 1928 offering called "town cabriolet," by which it really meant town *car* (a limousine with open chauffeur's compartment).

Perhaps the simplest definition is that a convertible is a car that converts from fully open to fully closed via a mechanism permanently affixed to it. And the converting part need not always be soft, as Ford proved with its famous late-Fifties "retractables."

Extremists sometimes insist that a true convertible must also have pillarless construction (no fixed B- and C-pillars) and be fully open (no structural members above the beltline except for the windshield, of course). But this would eliminate many prewar convertible sedans as well as postwar quirks like the 1949-51 Kaisers and Frazers and the 1950 Rambler (not to mention "targa" types like the 1968-82 Corvette). We won't go quite that far, as in the general context of engineering vocabulary, it would be wrong to do so. That its top folds back and windows roll down is enough to define a "true" convertible.

The definition must also include like-equipped two-seaters, though these have often been called "roadsters," even after their makers had given them convertible features. By our definition, the 1955-57 Thunderbird and open Corvettes after 1955 are genuine convertibles, too.

Let us be equally clear about our purpose here, which is to provide a general survey of American convertibles by decade. For brevity and to avoid duplication, this book does *not* attempt detailed descriptions of individual models. Readers seeking such information are referred to a previous work by Richard M. Langworth and the Auto Editors of CONSUMER GUIDE®, *The Encyclopedia of American Cars 1930-1980,* which covers convertibles as well their contemporary linemates. This book, however, does provide appendices listing convertible production figures by make and for the industry as a whole. The text provides pertinent facts on the design, engineering, performance, and other traits of a model or series, primarily as they relate to the convertible versions, of course.

Just when did convertibles begin? Careful reviews of body offerings indicate that they arrived in model year 1927. And contrary to earlier accounts, they were built by far more than two or three companies. Research discloses convertibles (or "cabriolets") in the 1927 lines of no fewer than eight manufacturers: Buick, Cadillac/LaSalle, Chrysler, duPont, Lincoln, Stearns, Whippet, and Willys.

So let us travel back in time and take up the breezy story of the American convertible at its birth.

1966 Cadillac Eldorado

1927–29

B I R T H   O F   A   L E G E N D

The Murphy-bodied 1929 Duesenberg Convertible Coupe (below) ranks as one of the most elegant ragtops ever built. Murphy also supplied coachwork for more attainable cars, such as this 1928 Hudson Convertible Landau Sedan (right).

*W*hile the origin of the convertible can be accurately traced to 1927, its inventor is somewhat less defined. Not, as one might suspect, because history has forgotten, but rather that it was the brainchild of many different minds.

As a matter of fact, no fewer than eight different carmakers debuted models that year which could be classified as convertibles. Furthermore, the manufacturing group was so diverse that their combined offerings spanned nearly the entire automotive spectrum in terms of both size and price.

Though the coincidence may seem extraordinary (and it was), analysis reveals that each of the companies possessed certain abilities or philosophies that prompted them to arrive at the same design conclusion. GM had literally invented the automotive styling profession; Chrysler was famous for its skilled body engineers; Lincoln, through the influence of Edsel Ford, was fashion-conscious; and E. Paul duPont was ever willing to adopt the latest design ideas. (However, his Model E, which offered his first convertibles, totaled only 83 chassis for all bodies; it's mentioned with the others mainly for historical completeness.)

The remaining three—Stearns, Whippet, and Willys— were all part of the John North Willys empire, where the convertible idea had long-standing appeal. Willys had bought Stearns (an established luxury-car producer) in December 1925, brought out Whippet as a "junior Willys" the following year, and had long offered a wide variety of Willys models with conventional and sleeve-valve engines to an enthusiastic

No fewer than eight different carmakers debuted models in 1927 that could be classified as convertibles.

Left: *LaSalle, introduced in 1927 as a "junior" Cadillac, offered one of the first convertibles in its debut year. For 1929, Buick offered this Model 54CC* (above)*, which sold for $1875.*

public. Throughout the Twenties, in fact, Willys-Overland never ranked below sixth in industry production and actually finished third in 1928, outpaced only by Chevrolet and Ford.

Thus it was that Willys-Overland listed numerous 2/4-passenger (rumble-seat) and four-passenger cabriolets under the Stearns-Knight, Whippet, Willys-Knight, and Willys banners in 1927-29, usually in cheap and expensive trim alike. Due to the onset of the Depression, however, the respected and luxurious Stearns vanished in 1929, followed by the Whippet in 1930. Although Willys continued as a carmaker until 1955, a convertible was never again offered in the lineup. Nevertheless, J.N. Willys deserves a good deal of credit for establishing the convertible early on in the low- and medium-priced fields, as well as at the upper end of the market.

Other manufacturers of convertibles or cabriolets in 1927 built them in rather limited numbers but, unlike Willys, were destined to keep building them a long time. Buick's sole convertible offering, the $1925 Master Six four-passenger convertible coupe, was one of the more popular early drop-tops, yet found fewer than 2400 buyers during that first model year. The volume for Cadillac's 2/4-passenger model (with an enclosed seat for two plus an open rumble for two more) is unrecorded but probably much lower, since at $3450 it cost a great deal more.

Chrysler's first convertible appeared in the new, *grand luxe* 1927 Imperial 80 series—a top-of-the-line two-seater whose roof folded via carriage-style landau irons. At $3495 it was outpriced that year only by the new Lincoln "Sport Convertible," a Brunn-bodied custom tagged at a cool $5000. A highlight of the bellwether New York Auto Salon in '27, this first Lincoln ragtop cost more than any other model in the line save an identically priced Dietrich phaeton.

Leaders quickly inspire imitators, and 1928 brought a

Oldsmobile offered this Viking convertible (left) in 1929. **Below:** *the very rare (and very expensive) DuPont Model G with body by Merrimac.* **Opposite:** *More affordable was this 1929 Studebaker Commander Six Convertible Cabriolet.*

The Society of Automotive Engineers defined a convertible as "any open car with roll-up windows," while progress in manufacturing and design ensured that convertible tops would be permanently attached to folding frameworks.

raft of new convertibles. Auburn, Franklin, Graham, Nash, Peerless, Studebaker, and Packard all had them; the pioneers, meantime, kept most of theirs going. Buick, however, now termed its convertible a "Country Club Coupe," the first of many flowery euphemisms by which builders tried to identify just what it was that they'd stumbled upon. Conversely, the 1928 Chryslers included a "Town Cabriolet" that was actually a town *car,* not a cabriolet.

Such confusing terminology may have prompted the Society of Automotive Engineers, the governing professional association of the car industry, to formally adopt "convertible" as a standard body designation. In its statement, the SAE was satisfied to define this as "any open car with roll-up windows,"

while progress in manufacturing and design insured that convertible tops would be permanently attached to folding frameworks that enabled easy raising and lowering.

This convenience was a large part of the convertible's early appeal, not to mention sales. Since the mid-Teens, the roadster and touring car, once the two most common open styles, had yielded in popularity to the closed "coach" and "sedan," which by the late Twenties were taking the bulk of sales industry-wide. Yet while fewer buyers still craved *al fresco* motoring, they were very much taken with the idea of tops that didn't need a small army to put up and down, and windows that got out of the way with only a couple turns of a crank.

Packard, then America's premier luxury make, moved quickly into the new field plowed by rivals Lincoln and Cadillac, issuing factory convertibles on all three of its 1928 chassis: Eight and Custom Eight ($6000-$6300) as well as the soon-to-vanish Six ($3650). Customers took to them, and Packard would continue listing a wide array of convertibles through 1942.

Auburn considered its "cabriolet" important enough to offer in five series, from price-leading 6-66 to the majestic eight-cylinder 115 on a 130-inch wheelbase. The latter, which could also be had as a roadster, phaeton, or speedster, was a handsome car. Advanced, too, with Bijur push-button chassis lubrication and Auburn's first hydraulic brakes, yet it cost only $2195. With lesser versions priced as low as $1295, Auburn soon commanded a large slice of the convertible market, though the company had never built in great volume—and never would.

Nash, regularly among the top 10 producers in these years, built many more convertibles than Auburn, leading off in 1928 with a pair of "convertible cabriolets" in Special and Standard guise selling for $2500-2600. These were pretty cars with classic upright styling, part of a Nash line that held over

3½ percent of the market that year—the best Nash would ever do until 1949.

Pioneering Chrysler switched its production cabriolet body to the mid-range Model 72 chassis in 1928, but Imperial buyers now had the choice of two custom-bodied convertibles: a LeBaron 2/4-seater (39 built) and a Dietrich convertible sedan (10 built at $6795, the very top of the line.) Though actual production figures aren't available, similarly low in volume but new for their makers were the Franklin Airman 3/5-passenger convertible ($2925), Graham-Paige's Senior Six and Model 835 Eight convertibles ($2185 and $2485, respectively), and a pair of 2/4-passenger rumble-seat cabriolets, the Fisher-bodied LaSalle ($2550) and Peerless 6-91 ($1895).

The more convenient new convertible style gained momentum in 1929 as Dodge, Hupmobile, Pontiac/Oakland, and Studebaker joined the fray. So did two very small producers, Blackhawk and Gardner. Dodge ragtops appeared in mid-1929 as a brace of cabriolets in the Senior Six line, and included such innovations as automatic windshield wipers, brake lights, bumpers front and rear, interior courtesy lights, and the first downdraft carburetor fitted to an American car.

Hupmobile, then enjoying one of its last prosperous years, settled on three models and a slightly different approach. Where most medium-priced convertibles were 2/4-passenger jobs with rumble seat, Hupp offered its small Six with a choice of bodies: one with a back seat, one without. The firm also offered full five-passenger capacity in its eight-cylinder Model M, after Buick's "Country Club" only the second five-passenger two-door convertible. As we know now, it was this configuration that would soon dominate convertible ranks.

Like many others, Pontiac extended its final run of 1928 cars into 1929, replacing them with "genuine" '29s early in the calendar year. Called the "New Big Six," this second series ushered in Pontiac's first convertible, a rumble-seat cabriolet selling for $845. The catalog described its finish as "Shadow

Dietrich-bodied Packard (below) spanned a 145.5-inch wheelbase and sold for $3350 in 1929—a princely sum. Packard vied for the luxury car crown with Cadillac and Lincoln, the latter of which offered this 1929 Model 167 Dietrich Convertible Sedan (right) for around $6000.

brown with orange trim striping and collapsible gray cloth teal top with tan mohair upholstery"—snappy. Other combinations were offered later. Some $400 upstream was an Oakland version with the same type body, though Pontiac's—with horizontal hood louvers and distinctive bisected radiator—looked nicer and sold better.

Studebaker was a serious convertible contender almost from the start. Winter 1927-28 brought announcement of Commander Regal and President State 2/4-passenger cabriolets with stylish bodywork and powerful engines, followed by a trio of four-seaters for a summer '28 revision (the new one was a Dictator Royal). South Bend also managed a little two-seat convertible coupe in its 108-inch-wheelbase Erskine line, one of the smallest of the new breed then available. Erskines never sold well, though, and the make would disappear in 1930.

Industry-leading Ford, at last returning to prosperity with the Model A, was the convertible's most important new adherent in 1929. At 16,421 units for the calendar year, its 2/4-passenger cabriolet beat the combined volume of all other new 1929 convertibles, making Dearborn the sales leader here, too. And so it would remain for most of the Thirties, building far more convertibles than anyone else—*including* Chevrolet, whose staid image didn't seem to suit the sporty body style. In fact, despite some beautiful early-Thirties body designs, Chevy wouldn't really be able to rival Ford's flathead ragtops for another 25 years.

Up to this point, roadsters, tourings, and phaetons had continued to take the lion's share of open-car sales, mainly because most every maker still had them, whereas only a few had thus far offered convertibles. But the lion's share wasn't what it had been. Ten years before, open cars took 90 percent of the total U.S. market; by 1929 they were at 10 percent. After 1930 their typical share was three percent or less, where it would remain through mid-decade; by that time, most of Detroit had simply given up on the outdated design.

The reason for that, of course, is that the convertible idea took hold. Though the process was gradual to be sure, it brought a merciless thinning in the ranks of other open styles. Signs of change were apparent as early as 1932, the last year that roadsters/tourings were more popular than convertibles. By 1939, convertibles outsold open cars 10 to one.

Still, the convertible had an uphill battle. It had barely come of age when America's greatest economic catastrophe set in, and though 17 nameplates listed convertibles for model year 1930, this relatively expensive and luxurious body style seemed out of place in a vastly diminished market. Economic necessity soon forced the more marginal manufacturers to drop convertibles as quickly as they'd embraced them. By decade's end, many of those companies were themselves gone for good.

The convertible survived, however, defying logic and the economic odds. The reasons it did—and some of its most splendid manifestations—are the subjects of our next chapter.

LaSalle continued its convertible for 1928 with this Fisher-bodied, 2/4 passenger rumble-seat cabriolet priced at $2550. It differed from the previous year's model in that the hood now sported 28 fine vertical louvers.

1930–39

DIAMONDS IN THE DARKNESS

*S*ome of the most stunning cars of this era (or any other, for that matter) originated through the efforts of Errett Lobban Cord. His automotive accomplishments, represented by Auburn, Cord, and Duesenberg, displayed the highest level of technology and elegance (and in some cases, even extravagance) seen from any automaker of the period. It comes as no surprise then, that all three makes sported convertible offerings by the beginning of the decade. Auburn, the humblest of the three, began producing convertibles in 1928. A year later, soft-tops were among the first Cords, the rakish L-29s, and Duesenberg followed shortly thereafter with custom-bodied examples.

E.L. Cord was to the Twenties what Lee Iacocca was to the Eighties. Having made his mark as a super salesman at the Moon agency in Chicago, he became president of ailing Auburn in 1926 at the age of only 32. Against all odds, he soon had Auburn back in the pink. By 1930, with visions of rivaling GM and Ford, he'd added Duesenberg, engine-maker Lycoming, two coachbuilders, and several other supplier companies to his budding empire.

Cord's automotive accomplishments, represented by Auburn, Cord, and Duesenburg, displayed the highest level of technology and elegance (and in some cases, even extravagance) seen from any automaker of the period.

Left: 1930 Essex Sun Sedan cost only $695, less than half that of Studebaker's 1931 President Four-Season Convertible Roadster (below). Note the Studebaker's lower pair of headlights, which turn with the front wheels.

A 113-bhp Vertical Eight powered the exclusive 1930 Stutz Model M convertible victoria by Rollston (right).

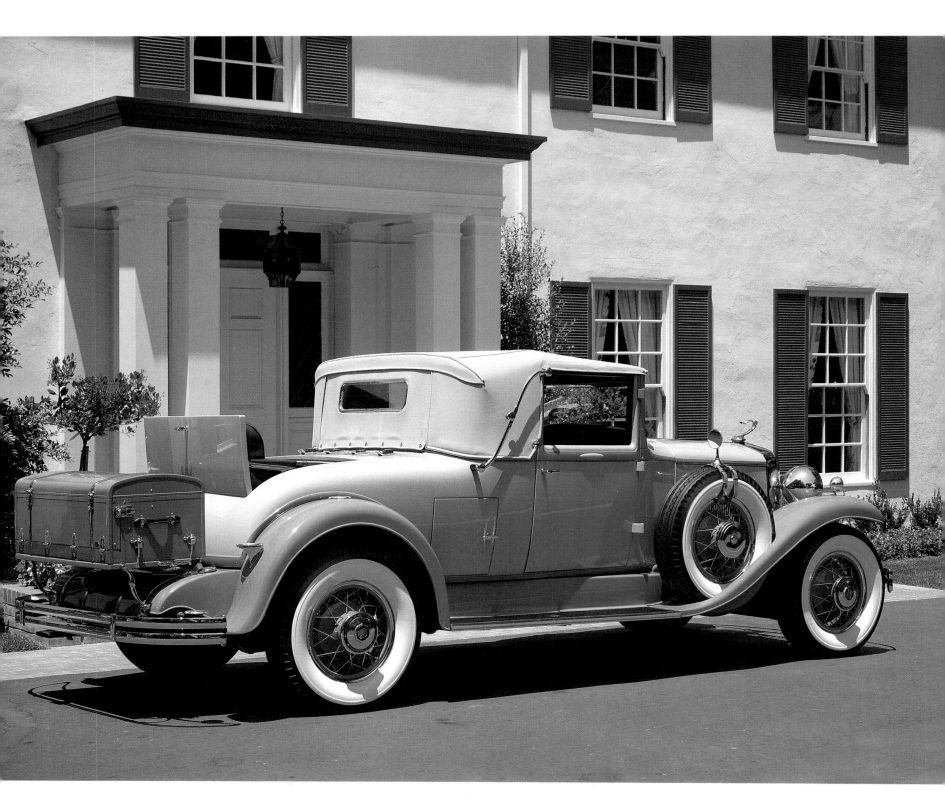

Cadillac's companion make, LaSalle, offered the 340 Convertible Coupe (above) for $2590 in 1930. Power for this near-4500 pound car was supplied by a 90-bhp, 340-cid V-8.

*Chrysler produced only 700 copies of
its CD convertible (below) in 1931.
Weighing in at about 3200 pounds, its
90-bhp straight eight provided more
than adequate performance for the day.*

But Auburn was always the linchpin of that dream, and Auburn's Twenties prosperity simply couldn't continue in the Thirties' Depression austerity. Though its cars were good-looking, fast, and bargain-priced, Auburn remained a relatively small automaker with too few dealers. Ultimately, E.L. Cord's mercurial management style created too many problems, and Auburn expired after 1936.

Nevertheless, like most of the other independents that didn't last this decade, Auburn built some of its finest cars in its final years. In fact, all Auburns from 1931 are certified Classics. Straight-eight power was Auburn's mainstay after 1930, with supercharged versions in 1935-36. But there was also the incredible 1932-34 Twelve—wretched excess for a troubled company but the cheapest V-12 in American history and, on its 133-inch wheelbase, an imposing car by any standard. Four-square styling characterized all Auburns through 1933, after which semi-streamlining took hold. Both remain pleasing to modern eyes.

The *crème de la crème* among open Auburns in this period, Gordon Buehrig's famous 1935-36 Speedster, is beyond our scope, but 2/4-passenger convertible cabriolets were listed in all series from 1931. Today they're hardly less scarce than Speedsters. Full model breakouts aren't available, but Auburn's total volume plunged from over 36,000 in 1931 to just 5500 registrations by '34. That means some pretty rare individual models, convertibles especially—true gold amidst the gloom of this failed marque. It was ever thus.

The Cord L-29 is equally rare and sought-after, though it's doubtful there are any left to find. E.L. created it to fill the yawning price chasm between Auburn and the exotic Duesenberg. The L-29 sported sensational good looks, in part due to its ultra-low stance; Indy race-car designer Harry Miller made that possible with his pioneering front-wheel drive system, adapted for production by Cornelius van Ranst.

Starting at $615, Chevy's 1931 Independence cabriolet (below) was very popular, as 23,077 were built that year. At the other end of GM's hierarchy was this 1931 Cadillac five-passenger All-Weather Phaeton (bottom), priced at around $3500.

Alan Leamy came up with truly classic lines of majestic proportions. The L-29 was stunning in any form, but the 2/4-passenger cabriolet and 5-seat phaeton sedan were naturally the most spectacular.

What they were not, however, was fast. With only a 115-horsepower Auburn straight eight to motivate it, the heavy—and *tail*-heavy—L-29 was none too good at climbing hills—or running fast on the flat. It wasn't cheap either, though prices were reduced after its 1929 debut to perk up sales. By 1931 the cabriolet was down from $3295 to $2495, the

phaeton to $2595. But sales didn't perk and production was halted in late '31 at about the 5000 mark. The Cord wasn't finished, though, and we'll return to it later.

A-C-D appropriately shunned "factory" bodies for the Duesenberg Model J, offering custom styles exclusively from the mighty car's 1928 announcement. As most every enthusiast knows, they were truly magnificent. Rollston (later Rollson) and LaGrande began offering convertible styles in 1930. Murphy, that paragon of West Coast flair, had actually built one or two convertible coupes and sedans on 1929-registered J chassis, though the majority came along in 1930-32.

There was nothing like a Duesie regardless of body, but it was truly without peer in open form. Fred Duesenberg's brains and E.L. Cord's money produced what they—and many others—called with no exaggeration "the world's finest motor

Chevy called its '32 line the Confederate, which included this $500 DeLuxe sport roadster, of which 8552 were produced. Note chromed side vents on hood and deeper headlight buckets.

car." One reason: its locomotive-like 420-cubic-inch Lycoming straight eight, with twin overhead camshafts driving four valves per cylinder to produce 265 horsepower—about twice the output of the industry's previous power leader, Chrysler. Equally imposing was the J's wheelbase: no less than 142.5 inches (sometimes stretched to 153.5 inches, though not for convertibles).

All Duesenberg Js were (and still are) the province of those *above* the "upper crust": stars rather than starlets, senators rather than congressmen, board chairmen rather than company presidents. More rarefied still were the customs you could count on fingers and toes: the long-wheelbase JN of Duesenberg's twilight years (sometimes with open bodywork), the thrilling supercharged SJ, and the legendary SSJ. The last saw only two examples, both LaGrande convertibles on abbreviated 125-inch chassis. The first was purchased off the showroom floor by film star Gary Cooper; the second was ordered by Clark Gable—probably because he couldn't bear the thought of being outclassed by friend "Coop." Both SSJs survive today—unquestionably among the most desirable and valuable American convertibles ever built.

No wonder. Only 470 Model J chassis were completed

Ford debuted its famous flathead V-8 in 1932, though this Model B cabriolet (top) carries the old four-cylinder engine. Above: 1932 Essex Pacemaker, built by Hudson, was priced at $845; nearly $300 more than the Ford.

The Depression took a heavy toll on all automakers, but Packard was still building genuine luxury cars, like this 1932 model.

Above: *1932 Auburn Eight, a 100-bhp performance bargain at $795. The 1932 Stutz Model DV32 Bearcat (right) boasted Weymann fabric bodywork aft of the cowl, and a 161-bhp, 32-valve straight eight in front of it.*

DeSoto's 1932 New Six Custom roadster, priced at $775, saw only 894 copies. A 211-cid inline six provided 75-bhp to move the car's 2748-pound heft.

between 1928 and 1936. Though a high proportion originally carried convertible bodies, there are more soft-top models now because of blatant body switching. Predictably, the company never made money with this formidable—and formidably expensive—masterpiece. But as Ken Purdy wrote, Fred Duesenberg had chosen "a good course and held unswervingly to it...With his mind and his two good hands, he had created something new and good and, in its way, immortal. And the creator is, when all is said and done, the most fortunate of men."

At the other end of the scale, the convertible began figuring into the dogfight between Ford and Chevrolet for the title of "USA 1." With the introduction of the Model A in 1928, Ford managed to wrestle the sales lead from Bill Knudsen's surging Chevy, only to lose it again in 1931. Not until the advent of the V-8 line in 1932 would Dearborn head off Knudsen's car, and then only for a few years.

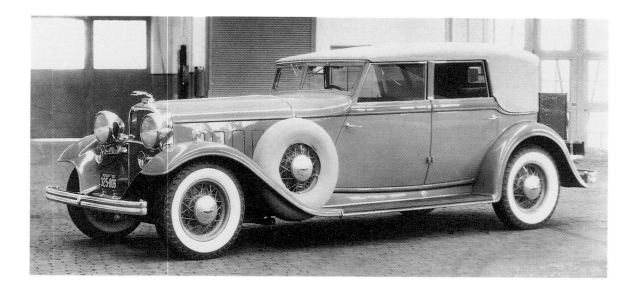

This 1932 Lincoln convertible sedan (right), *with body by Dietrich, sits on a 145-inch wheelbase and is powered by a 448-cid V-12 producing 150 bhp.*

1932 Nash Model 981 convertible sedan (right) *carried a "Twin Ignition" inline eight that sported two spark plugs per cylinder and produced 94-bhp. Price was $1325.*

Offered in small numbers beginning in the A's second year, the jaunty 2/4-passenger convertible cabriolet was an established part of the Ford line by 1931. (Unlike most other body styles, however, it would be available only in standard trim through 1937, when it became a better-equipped DeLuxe.) Chevy, which had no counterpart before then, brought out a 2/4-passenger rumble-seat cabriolet in that year's new "Independence" series. At $595 and $615 respectively, both these cars were pricey, though not top of the line. Ford also offered true convertible sedans, priced at $640 each; Chevy countered with two-door landau phaetons at $650 a copy.

Whereas Chevy sold nearly twice as many cabriolets as Ford in 1931, the tables were turned the following year with the advent of the Ford V-8. By 1934, it wasn't even close; Ford's cabriolet outsold Chevy's almost four to one. Chevrolet furloughed its cabriolet for 1935, then revived it in the restyled '36 fleet. Nevertheless, the model continued selling poorly. Ford did much better, however, and even continued convertible sedans (which Chevy never bothered with) through 1939. Dearborn's speedy V-8 was clearly preferred by soft-top buyers—in retrospect, hardly surprising.

Even before the 1929 stock-market crash, the Big Two had a rival in Chrysler Corporation. Founded by Walter P. Chrysler in 1924, it soon became a "full-line" producer with the 1928 acquisition of Dodge Brothers and the introduction of Plymouth and DeSoto that same year. Well known for

handsome styling in its early days, the Highland Park company had been an early advocate of convertibles. Dodge and Chrysler had them in the Twenties. Plymouth and DeSoto got them in 1930.

A hotly competitive new Plymouth appeared for 1931, still with a four-cylinder engine but outclassing its rivals with "Floating Power"—an arrangement whereby the engine was suspended along its center of gravity using mounts lined with heavy rubber to insulate them from the frame—a simple but remarkable innovation that gave Plymouth "the smoothness of an eight and the economy of a four." Chrysler's low-price make finished third in production for the first time that year and would remain there for the next quarter-century, aided by a switch from fours to sixes effective with the '33s.

Plymouth fielded Standard and DeLuxe series from 1932, and it initially issued convertibles in both. This was a shrewd departure from Ford/Chevy tactics, and it worked. While Chevy struggled to sell convertibles, Plymouth's slightly better-heeled customers took about 7000 a year in 1932-33. Then Plymouth restricted its ragtop to the DeLuxe line for 1934 and sales fell apart—curious, because the DeLuxe had previously outsold the Standard version. Successive restyles, attractive colors, and handsome leather interiors didn't seem to help. In 1937, with the industry fast recovering from the Depression, Plymouth moved only 3110 convertibles.

As an experiment, Plymouth built a number of convertible

sedans for 1932, but didn't field a production model until 1939. It was only a one-year stand and just 387 were built—Chrysler Corporation's last four-door convertible. Its demise coincided with that of the great Walter Chrysler, who'd been ailing for several years. He died in 1940 of a cerebral hemorrhage at age 65. Many say the company's soul died with him, but some of the firm's finest hours lay ahead in the Fifties, Sixties, and Eighties.

DeSoto and Dodge, Chrysler's mid-range makes, offered small numbers of convertibles throughout the Thirties. The sole exception was the '34 DeSoto line, which relied exclusively on the advanced but controversial Airflow design that wasn't conceived with a drop-top in mind. (It was just as well. The

This 1932 LaSalle convertible coupe weighed in at a hefty 4630 pounds. Priced at $2545, it was powered by a 115-bhp V-8 of 353-cid that it had inherited from the Cadillac line.

Built on a 117-inch wheelbase and powered by an 80-bhp inline six, the model 55 Six convertible sedan (below) represented the bottom of the Studebaker line for 1932. Also offered were Dictator, Commander, and President Eights on wheelbases up to 135 inches.

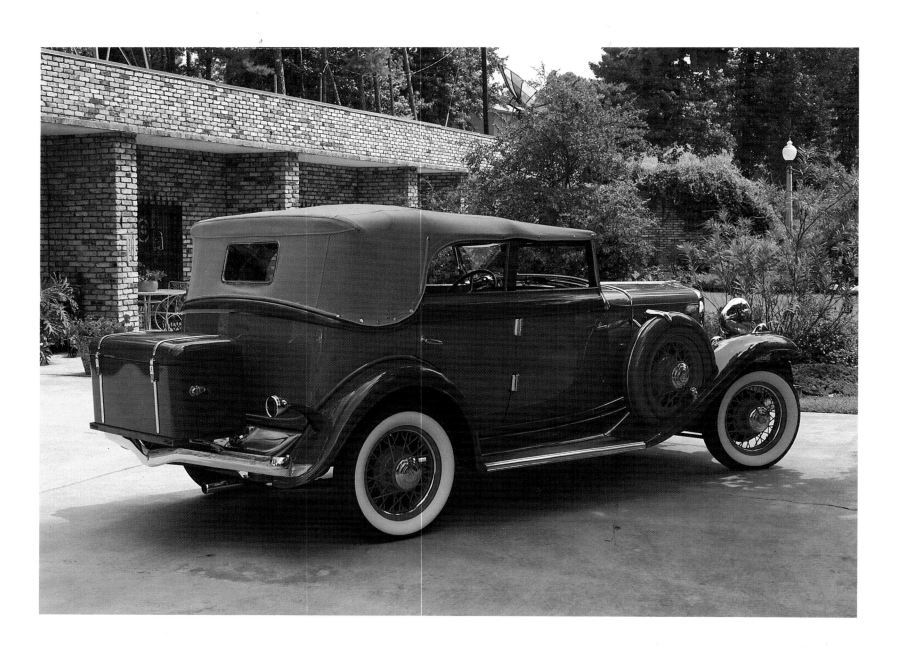

This 1933 convertible roadster (right) is representative of the last Nashes that displayed "upright" styling.

Stylish and fast, the 1933 Essex Terraplane Deluxe Eight convertible coupe (above) *cost but $765.*

Airflow wouldn't have made a nice-looking convertible, and the body style just didn't fit the project goals of superior aerodynamics and all-steel "safety" construction, both of which were more readily accomplished with closed bodies.)

As is widely known, the Airflow never got off the ground. But contrary to long-accepted "wisdom," the reason was not so much styling (which many buyers liked) as production delays and unfounded rumors (some abetted by an envious GM), both of which dampened initial interest and started thoughts that the Airflow was a "lemon." DeSoto thus managed only 14,000 model-year sales, prompting a hasty regrouping around more conventional Airstream styling for 1935.

Not that DeSoto had shown much flair for convertibles.

31

Weighing close to three tons, this 1933 Cadillac is powered by the company's mammoth 452-cid, 165-bhp "sweet sixteen."

Its open models were among the dullest around—if that's possible—though they cost close to $1000 and came in the more deluxe of two series. With its 1936 restyle, DeSoto attempted a convertible sedan that cost well over $1000 and thus sold poorly: 215 that year, 426 the next, and just 88 in 1938, after which it was dropped. Perhaps as a result, DeSoto opted out of the soft-top business for 1939, then returned permanently with a convertible coupe in the handsome Ray Dietrich-styled 1940 line.

Dodge offered far more ragtops. In 1933, for example, it had no fewer than four, including a convertible sedan, all with a choice of six or eight cylinders. But the threadbare Thirties market demanded only about 1600 of them—hardly profitable.

Below: *Stutz produced this racy DV32 convertible coupe in 1933, the same year Buick offered the Model 88C convertible phaeton (bottom).*

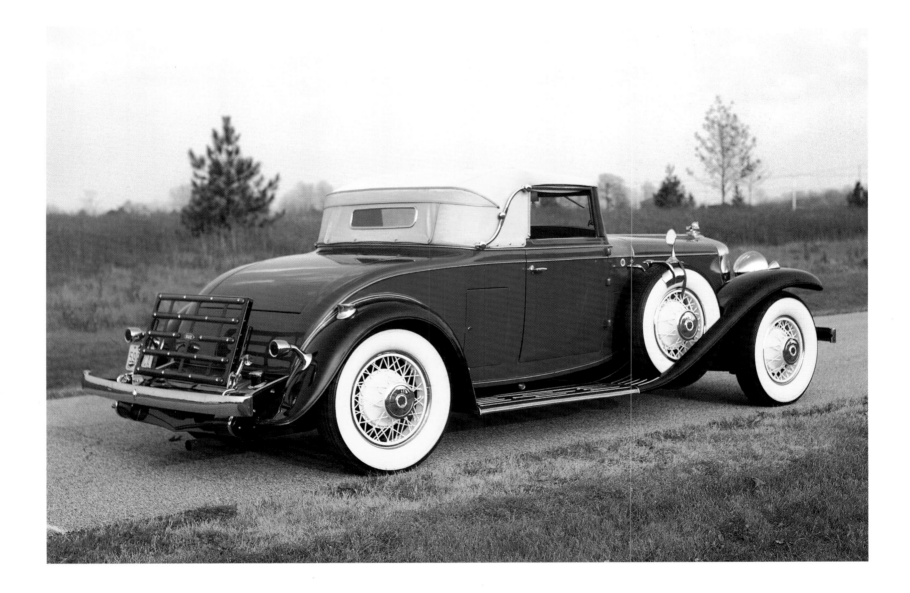

1934 Cadillac V-8 convertible sedan

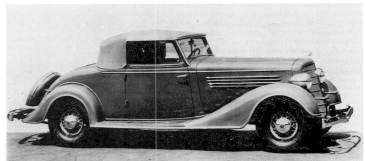

*Packard produced only 960
12-cylinder cars in 1934, one
of which is shown at left.* **Below:**
*1934 Buick Series 60 convertible
coupe sported a 100-bhp V-8, but
only 263 were sold at $1495.*

Accordingly, the division dropped its straight-eight lines for
'34, built diminishing numbers of convertible sedans (none
after 1938) and, like DeSoto, forgot soft-tops entirely for
1939 (which probably accounts for that year's Plymouth
convertible sedan).

Long overlooked among Classic-era convertibles are the
singular Chryslers of 1931-33. If Chryslers were handsome
before, stylist Herb Weissinger made them real head-turners
with his unabashed copying of the Cord L-29. The similarity
was most striking in the smoothly curved vertical-bar radiators
of the top-line Imperial and mid-range Eight/DeLuxe Eight,
though the Cord's deft overall proportions and artful
"clamshell" fenderlines were also in evidence.

Chrysler offered rumble-seat convertible coupes in each of
its four series for 1931-33, and added convertible sedans with
1932's mid-year "second series" lineup. (A four-door convertible
also appeared in the '31 Imperial CG series, though only 25
were built.) The 1933s were mildly altered in engine and
wheelbase assignments and gained radiators tilted back a
little, but their basic design remained largely intact.

1934 Auburn Eight cabriolet

Clockwise, from above: *1934 Dodge Deluxe Six convertible coupe, 1934 Ford Deluxe, 1934 Lincoln V-12 convertible coupe, 1934 Cadillac convertible coupe.*

A good thing too, for these were stylish cars, particularly in topless form, and smooth performers. The big straight-eight Imperials were the most impressive, of course, their long wheelbases (126-146 inches) making the most of what Weissinger had wrought. They were fully worthy of comparison with other Classics except in technical complexity—and price, which ranged from just $1325 for the 1933 Imperial Eight convertible coupe to a reasonable $3500 or so for LeBaron semi-custom styles. Other coachbuilders crafted one-off or few-at-a-time styles for various Chrysler chassis in these years, including Waterhouse in America and even a few European shops (the latter tending toward the more common Six and Eight platforms).

Having abandoned roadsters and phaetons after 1931, Chrysler joined DeSoto in 1934's Airflow debacle, though it didn't suffer as much because division managers had decided to retain the conventionally styled Six at the bottom of the line (a hedge, perhaps, but prudent, as events would show).

For those intrigued by statistics, the Thirties were a time of stability for the convertible coupe and sedan, which had long since become "specialty models." Open cars of all types shrunk from a dominant 83-percent market share in 1920 to just 10 percent by '29. In the Depression years they accounted for about three percent of total sales, about one percent after 1936.

Buick asked just $1495 for this 1935 Series 60 convertible coupe, yet only 111 were built.

This offered Chrysler's only folding-roof models that year: the Six convertible coupe ($815) and Custom Six convertible sedan ($970). Like DeSoto, Chrysler toned down Airflows for '35 with less radical styling, but with eight as well as six cylinders (DeSoto was strictly sixes in this period). Convertible coupes and sedans arrived only as Eights, but the Airflow's steady decline prompted the addition of six-cylinder versions for '36.

The Airflow bowed out after 1937, the year other Chryslers were restyled with ungainly barrel-like fronts. The '38 fleet brought the return of non-Airflow Imperials and Eights, but other models were only a bit less awkward than they'd been the previous year. Much smoother lines marked the all-new '39s—but there were no convertibles. Instead, Chrysler emphasized coupes and sedans with fancy trim and, for the Hayes-bodied Victoria, distinctive rooflines. But the absence was only temporary, and convertible coupes would return for 1940.

For those intrigued by statistics, the Thirties were a time of stability for the convertible coupe and sedan, which had long since become "specialty models." Open cars of all types shrunk from a dominant 83-percent market share in 1920 to just 10 percent by '29. In the Depression years they accounted

Ford reinstated its convertible sedan for 1935 (above), pricing it at $750. 4234 were built. Left: 1935 LaSalle convertible coupe.

Right: *Pontiac offered both six- and eight-cylinder cabriolets for 1935, at $775 and $840, respectively.*

for about three percent of total sales, about one percent after 1936 according to the National Automobile Chamber of Commerce (though the latter apparently included roadsters and touring cars, making the actual market penetration for true convertibles even less). Convertibles then recovered to 2-3 percent through decade's end; about 95 percent were two-doors.

With all this, you might wonder how convertibles survived past the Thirties. Since more were offered during the depths of the Depression than in recovery 1936-37 and 1939-40, they were clearly on the wane by mid-decade, the four-door in particular. (Some low-volume independents even lost money on them.) The reason isn't hard to divine: growing buyer preference for the greater safety and comfort of closed bodies, which advanced rapidly in the Thirties via features like all-steel construction, integral trunks, and door ventwings for "no-draft" ventilation. Still, the convertible did not die.

Why? The answer seems to be the perennial one long advanced by its proponents: The convertible was needed— not for profits as much as sheer sales-appeal, and the luster it lent to the workaday models standing next to it on showroom floors. The convertible was a symbol: always the best, the most luxurious, the most costly model in each maker's line, from Chevrolet to Cadillac, Lincoln to Ford. And remembering

The 1934 Buick Series 60 convertible phaeton (left) offered 100-bhp for its $1675 price, but the four-door ragtop was beginning to fade in popularity; only 575 were built.

Above: 1935 Studebaker Commander Eight offered 107-bhp for about $1000. Cadillac's V-8 convertible coupe (right) boasted 130-bhp, but prices started at $2445.

that most people were struggling with the mere basics of life at the time, the convertible served the important psychological purpose of assuring them that happy days would indeed be here again. In other words, the convertible ultimately became something to live for; a romantic reward for the hard times now endured. Hope meant much in the Thirties—about the only currency many folks had.

General Motors, grounded for a decade on Alfred Sloan's marketing dictum of "a car for every purse and pocketbook" and thus the master at parting money from consumers, continued to offer more convertibles than most anyone else—and more variety within each of its makes. The glamorous convertible sedan (which GM usually called "convertible phaeton") was another of the firm's stocks-in-trade (except at Chevrolet). Of course, GM had more employee mouths to feed and thus perhaps needed the allure of convertibles more than, say, Studebaker, whose sales tended to rely more on buyer loyalty than outright value for money or even innovative styling and engineering.

As noted (Chapter I), Cadillac and LaSalle, GM's top-line makes, had been among the first with true convertibles in the late Twenties. Cadillac's fabulous Sixteens and Twelves were offered with a vast array of factory and custom bodies, including convertibles as a matter of course. There was always a convertible coupe in Cadillac's "basic" eight-cylinder line, usually priced competitively. The 1933 edition, for example, cost $2845, just $50 above the relatively spartan roadster—though both represented a good year's pay for the average worker.

But it's the big multi-cylinder Cadillacs that everyone remembers, perhaps because these models were relatively uncommon after 1930-31, when they sold about 9000 units combined. Staggeringly expensive, they seemed almost vulgar in an era of widespread misery. (Other big luxury cars were shunned for the same reason. Even many of those who bought them often drove around in something less pretentious). Later, their engines were outmoded by advancing technology. For example, the introduction of precision-insert rod bearings helped eliminate the knock and high-speed engine wear that originally enticed wealthy types away from eights. Cadillac's Twelve thus vanished after 1937; the Sixteen somehow managed to hang on through 1940, though it seemed a relic of another age by then.

Nineteen thirty-four brought a deftly restyled Cadillac

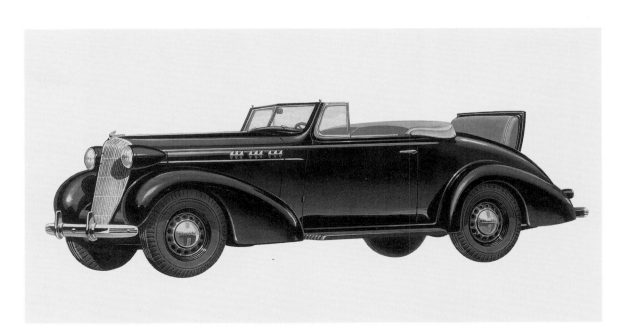

Chevy never bothered with convertible
sedans, but Ford did; this 1936 model
was equipped with the famous flathead
V-8 producing 90-bhp. 5601 were built.

Also available from Ford that year
was the popular Deluxe cabriolet
(right), of which 14,068 were built.

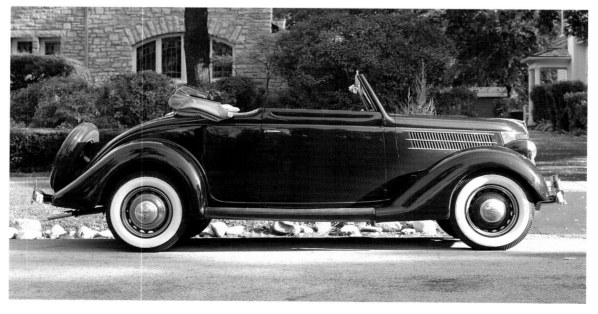

and a new LaSalle. The latter, born in 1927 as a junior Caddy with a smaller V-8, now became a sort of glorified Buick: cut $1000 in price, given an Oldsmobile L-head straight eight and, to its credit, GM's new "Knee-Action" independent front suspension. At least it looked somewhat like the smoother, more modern new Caddy. The LaSalle two-passenger convertible coupe, a glorious expression of money-talks class consciousness in 1933, had sold for about $3000 over the previous few years. The 2/4-passenger convertible of 1934 sold for $1695, same as the four-door sedan (suggesting GM purposely took a loss on it). Better still, it weighed 700 pounds less, to the benefit of performance.

LaSalle retained convertible coupes for the rest of the decade. Convertible sedans were also available from 1937, when Cadillac power returned. Prices were cut further in later years to encourage sales. The soft-top was down to $1255 by 1936, a long way from the heady sums of 1927-33. But Cadillac's medium-price Depression-fighter was a terminal case, being slowly squeezed out of its market by Buick as the economy inched toward recovery. LaSalle's last hurrah came

with the 1940 models, again adroitly styled by GM's Harley Earl. In some ways, they were the best LaSalles since the originals.

Buick, Olds, and Pontiac fared better than LaSalle, both generally and with convertibles. Buick was GM's convertible king, largely because it covered the widest market in the company. By 1931 the division was established with a four-series lineup (50, 60, 80, and 90) spanning $1000-$2000—which was quite a span in those days. Two years later it had a convertible in each line save the Series 90, which got one for '34. With the '36s came the now-familiar Special, Century, Roadmaster, and Limited names. By that point, Buick usually offered five or six convertible models a year, including four-door "phaetons" in the two senior series, plus Special and Century versions in 1937-38.

For most of the decade, Buick's annual soft-top production was 3000-5000 units, the majority being Special and Century convertible coupes. Phaetons were discarded after 1938 and saw far fewer copies.

Oldsmobile and Pontiac, with narrower market assignments

The "down market" One Twenty helped Packard survive the Depression years. Yet despite representing the bottom of the line for 1936, this convertible coupe was a snappy car that started at only $1110.

One of the most recognizable cars of the Thirties, this 1936 "coffin nose" Cord came with front-wheel drive, four-speed gearbox with electric pre-selector, and hidden headlamps.

and considerably trimmed lineups after 1933, built fewer soft-tops in this period. Nevertheless, Olds fielded at least one convertible in each series each year save 1934, when an eight-cylinder model was its lone entry. Pontiac offered but a single six-cylinder series in 1931, added a V-8 line for '32 (an extension of recently deceased Oakland), then went to straight eights for 1933-34. Each of these contained a convertible. Pontiac then blossomed into two Sixes and an Eight for 1935-36, each with a version of what it called a 2/4-passenger cabriolet.

In strict Sloan fashion, Pontiac convertibles usually sold for $800-$900, Oldsmobiles for about $900-$1100; this at a time when $100-$200 was a big difference. We should also not forget that Oakland, Pontiac's parent, had a convertible in its swan song '31 line, priced at $995.

Unlike Buick, Pontiac and Olds bothered with convertible sedans only from time to time: Pontiac in 1937-38, Olds in the big 98 series of 1940-41. The latter was impressive on its 125-inch wheelbase and cost the world for an Oldsmobile: about $1600. This may explain why production ran to only 50 units

Chevy brought back its cabriolet for 1936 (above), after a one-year absence. Sales were slow, however, as low-priced buyers preferred Ford's V-8. Left: 1936 Hudson Eight convertible coupe sold for $875 in the Deluxe series, $970 in Custom guise.

For 1936, Pontiac offered a cabriolet in three series: six-cylinder Master ($760) and Deluxe ($810) Silver Streak, and Deluxe Eight Silver Streak ($855).

Cadillac offered a Series 70 V-8 ($2745) and Series 80 V-12 ($3445) convertible sedan on the same 131-inch wheelbase for 1936.

in the first year and 119 in the second.

The big guns among Thirties independents were Hudson (helped immeasurably by its offshoot Essex and Terraplane makes), Studebaker (when not in receivership), and Packard (after 1935, when it became a volume manufacturer by dint of the successful, lower-priced One Twenty). Hudson had popularized the closed coach as an Essex model in the Twenties, but stuck with the traditional roadster and touring until 1932, when it finally switched to convertibles for both the Hudson and Essex lines.

The big Hudson changed as dramatically as LaSalle once the Depression set in. Volume plummeted from a rollicking 300,000 units in 1929 to barely 40,000 four years later. Handsome and exciting though they were, the top-line Hudsons just wouldn't sell. Adding insult to injury, Biddle & Smart, the make's long-time coachbuilder, was forced to close in 1930. Hudson's classic four-square styling ended three years later, accompanied by the return of six-cylinder power. Transitional 1934-35 models were followed by very modern, all-new '36s with skirted fenders, tall and rounded die-cast grilles, and all-steel bodies.

Hudson limited itself to a single convertible in 1932-33, then listed one or more in most series. By 1938, convertible coupes and broughams were offered in a reabsorbed Terraplane line (DeLuxe and Super models) as well as in the senior 112, Custom Six, and Deluxe Eight series. All were two-doors. Convertible coupes had a single bench seat for three; broughams were conventional six-seaters.

The low-priced Essex had helped Hudson rise as high as third in the industry in 1927, but couldn't sustain itself after the Great Crash. What kept Hudson going was the smart and speedy Terraplane, which was an Essex model in 1932-33, a separate make in 1934-37, and a Hudson series in 1938 (after which the name was discarded). Terraplanes would generally do up to 80 mph and 25 miles per gallon yet cost as little as $425, though convertibles were priced almost $200 higher. Adding to its appeal was an extra-cost eight-cylinder evolution of the original Essex Six, offered beginning in 1933.

The first Essex convertibles, Pacemaker and Terraplane, arrived for 1932. All Essex models were called Terraplane the following year, when a convertible was cataloged in each of the line's five series. Models were then cut and the Eight

Oldsmobile offered two convertible coupes for 1937: one with a six ($965), the other, shown at left, with an eight ($1080).

dropped as Essex disappeared and Terraplane became a separate make, but there were usually two convertible coupes each year and, in 1937, convertible broughams too. Of course, the open cars sold for much more than the average Terraplane: $725-$845 in 1937, for example, when closed cars started at $595. But their numbers and variety reflected well on the Terraplane's sporty and youthful personality.

Studebaker entered the Thirties with a broad lineup, though the economic malaise soon caused the deletion of a good many models. It also nearly wiped out Studebaker. By 1933, the successive failures of side ventures Erskine and Rockne plus the purchase of Pierce-Arrow had put the old firm in receivership. Production executive Harold Vance and sales vice president Paul Hoffman labored to pull it out, dumping Pierce and rebuilding the company's credit while working on more saleable cars.

Another of the famous "coffin nose" Cords (above), this one a '37. Cabriolet prices ranged from $2595 for the standard 812, to $3010 for supercharged versions.

The Studebaker line was down to only three series by 1934: Dictator Six, and Commander and President Eight. But this is misleading, for each comprised several sub-series: standard, Regal, St. Regis, and Custom, plus the restyled "Year Ahead" '35 models that arrived in July 1934. Vance and Hoffman were concentrating on volume sellers, so there were "just" six convertibles: standard and Regal versions in each main line. But with only minimal demand, all were dropped for 1936, reflecting the continuing need for greater standardization and reduced production costs.

Meantime, Studebaker was planning the Champion, the low-price car that would return it to financial health in 1939. Still, this and other models would appear only as coupes and sedans, and with one brief exception, Studebaker would build nothing but closed cars through 1946.

But that exception was a dandy: a convertible sedan in the 1938-39 Commander and President series. Big and impressive, it sold for a whopping $300-$350 more than the next costliest model in each line. The predictable results were meager sales and very low production, making these some of the rarest and most desirable prewar Studeys for today's collectors.

Studebaker's future partner Packard probably experienced the greatest image change of any independent in the Thirties. From a maker of luxury cars "for a discriminating clientele," Packard moved gingerly downmarket with the Light Eight of 1932, then aggressively with the One Twenty of 1935 and the Six of 1937. These do-or-die medium-price models not only saved the company's hide but made Packard a significant contender in the annual production race for the first time. From its accustomed 18th place and an almost negligible 4803 units in 1933, Packard leaped to a strong eighth and a record 123,000 cars by 1937. The One Twenty ("Eight" in 1938), accompanied by the Packard Six after 1936, accounted for well over 90 percent of production. Both were offered as convertible coupes. The One Twenty was also available as a convertible sedan—about which hangs an interesting tale.

One Twenty convertible sedans carried a body plate reading "Dietrich," and many concluded that the great coachbuilder who'd created so many magnificent senior-Packard bodies in

Studebaker's future partner Packard probably experienced the greatest image change of any independent in the Thirties. From a maker of luxury cars "for a discriminating clientele," Packard moved gingerly downmarket in 1932.

One of the few GM convertible sedans offered in 1937, this Pontiac Deluxe Eight sold for $1235; six-cylinder versions went for $1197.

past years was responsible. This was precisely Packard's intent, but there was no connection. Ray Dietrich had left Dietrich, Inc., in 1930; by the time the One Twenty appeared, he was working on 1937-38 models for Walter Chrysler. But Murray had absorbed Dietrich, Inc., and continued to use the name. "Some of my leftover designs were actually completed by Murray and that's how the name went on the cars," Dietrich said later. "But I don't remember any lines of mine on a One Twenty. Murray, however, had established the practice by now, and they went ahead with it. How could I fight the Packard Motor Car Company? I had to trust their honesty, figuring there was honesty among thieves. But if they stole my name, I was very happy. The publicity didn't hurt!"

Packard naturally offered convertible coupes on its senior Eight and Twelve chassis throughout the decade, though they were a very small percentage of a total volume that itself was

Left: 1937 Oldsmobile Six convertible coupe cost $965; an eight-cylinder version cost $1080. Production was 1619 and 728, respectively.

Packard offered this One-Twenty convertible coupe in 1937 for $1060. It came with a 120-bhp straight eight on a 120-inch wheelbase. Other Packard ragtops were the Six ($910), Super Eight ($2680), and Twelve ($3450).

With a 175-bhp V-12 propelling its 5255-pound heft, the mighty 1937 Packard Twelve convertible coupe (right) provided almost obscene open-air luxury for four. Below: At $1350, the 1937 LaSalle convertible coupe was a rival to Packard's One Twenty.

small. Record 1937, for example, produced 115,500 Sixes and
One Twentys against 5793 Super Eights and 1300 Twelves.
The grand old Twelve, once queen of the line and a standard
for America, vanished after model year 1939 when only 446
were sold.

Among the smaller independents, Willys built no convertibles
after 1930, while Hupp and Graham (formerly Graham-Paige)
produced a handful and Nash rather more. Hupp had its best
year ever in 1928, registering over 50,000 cars, but wouldn't
reach five figures after 1932 despite Raymond Loewy's
handsome and advanced 1934 "Aerodynamic" design. The
firm took a hiatus in mid-1936, reopened fitfully in 1937-38,
then closed for good.

Hupp released its first convertibles in 1929 and generally
had one in each series each year, variously calling it convertible
coupe, convertible cabriolet, and roadster cabriolet. Hupp's
last convertibles appeared in conventionally styled six- and
eight-cylinder series for 1934.

Graham, whose history parallels Hupp's, dropped all its
soft-top models after 1937. This automaker also had its best
year before the Depression, then entered the Thirties with too
many models for the shrunken market: sixes and eights in five
series. Sales were down to 20,000 by 1931, then dropped by
half over the next two years.

Graham produced its best convertibles in its leanest years.
Notable was the Blue Streak Eight of 1932, beautifully sculpted
by Amos Northup, creator of the '31 Reo Royale. The Blue
Streak's skirted fenders prefigured an industry trend, and its
245-cid straight eight boasted an advanced aluminum cylinder
head. The convertible, a 2/4-seater, came only in DeLuxe

*At close to $3500, this 1938
Cadillac convertible coupe (left)
was out of the reach of most
ragtop buyers; less than 100
were built.*

Above: 1938 Lincoln Zephyr carried a 110-bhp V-12 and sold for $1700. 600 were built. Right: 1938 Cadillac Series 75 convertible sedan boasted a 140-bhp V-8; 58 were built.

Nash offered this Ambassador Six convertible cabriolet (right) in 1938 for $1099.

1938 Buick Series 60 Century convertible coupe (right) was equipped with the firm's biggest straight eight; 320-cid, 141-bhp. It sold for $1359.

trim for 1932; a Standard model was added for 1933-34 along with six-cylinder running mates.

Also for 1934, Graham unleashed the Supercharged Custom Eight, America's first popular-price "hyperaspirated" car, packing 135 horsepower. Over the next six years, Graham would build more blown production cars than anyone else before, but it wasn't enough to insure the future. The 1936 line comprised sixes only, normal and supercharged, including standard and Custom Supercharger convertibles. These continued through 1937, after which Graham abandoned soft-tops and pinned its hopes—in vain, as it turned out— on the odd "Spirit of Motion" design now widely known as the "Sharknose."

Packard offered six-, eight-, and 12-cylinder convertibles in 1938. Above is an Eight convertible coupe, which boasted 120-bhp and sold for $1365.

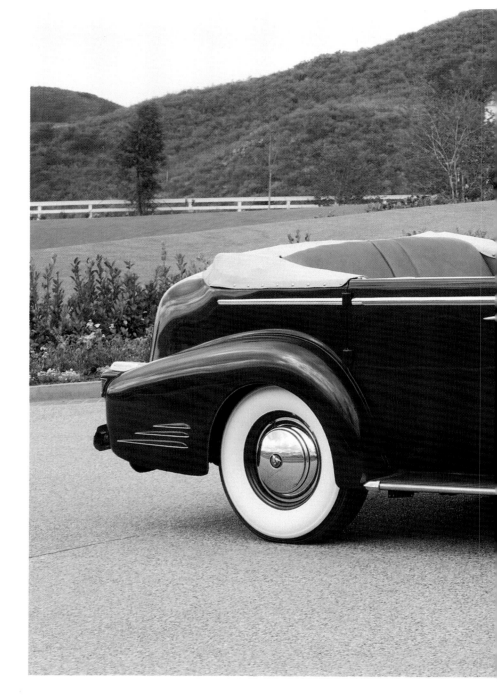

Mention of the last Hupps and Grahams inevitably leads us to the second and final Cord, the great 810/812 of 1936-37. Bodies for the abortive rear-drive Hupp Skylark/Graham Hollywood of 1940-41 were made using dies obtained after Cord Corporation's collapse, but all were sedans; the 810/812 convertibles weren't similarly reincarnated (except for a prototype Skylark).

Like its L-29 predecessor, the 810 employed front-wheel drive but was far more compact and maneuverable, thanks to a Lycoming V-8 with 115 bhp. The 1937 model 812 was little changed apart from optional availability of a Schwitzer-Cummins supercharger that boosted power to 170—an astounding 190 with the "high-boost" package. So equipped, an 812 would do nearly 110 mph and 0-60 mph in 13 seconds, which made it among the fastest of prewar American cars.

But the second-generation Cords are mainly remembered for their predictive, Gordon Buehrig styling—smooth "coffin-nose" hood, wrapped "venetian blind" radiator louvers, graceful body lines. There were innovations aplenty: the industry's first concealed headlamps and fuel filler, dual taillights, a separate license-plate lamp, and full wheel covers. All were advanced for the day and particularly heartening after the grim early Thirties.

There were two 810/812 convertibles, both two-doors: the aptly named Sportsman, a two-seat cabriolet, and a four-passenger four-window "convertible sedan" called Phaeton. They were relative bargains, too, at about $2600. Alas, production delays and mechanical woes doomed Cord's comeback, and relatively few 810/812s were sold.

Nash was one of the handful of independents that would survive these difficult years. It did so by merging with the Kelvinator appliance firm in 1937, which brought a bonus in the person of Kelvinator's cigar-chomping president, George Mason. Though founder Charles W. Nash remained nominally in charge, Mason increasingly made the decisions. They were usually the right ones.

Early-Thirties Nashes were sumptuous, beautifully styled cars with many special features. Notable was "Twin Ignition," meaning two sets of spark plugs/points/condensers/coils operating from a single distributor; overhead valves, an idea Charlie Nash probably got when he managed Buick; and nine main bearings for all straight eights. Styling was classically upright through 1933. A more streamlined group of '34s previewed 1935's still-swoopier "Aero-form" design with rounded lines and pontoon fenders. Successive facelifts belied its promise, however, and Nashes weren't really pretty again until 1939, appearing with flush-fit headlights and a slim

vertical prow flanked by short, square grilles.

Through 1934, Nash soft-tops were conventional rumble-seat cabriolets and convertible sedans. Convertibles vanished with the '35 restyle (and a drastic, Depression-inspired model cutback), but an appropriately smooth 3/5-passenger cabriolet joined the '37 line, offered as a low-price Lafayette 400 and as a plush Ambassador Six and Eight. For many enthusiasts, the fine-looking '39 Ambassador Eight, on the longest (125-inch) wheelbase, is the most desirable late-prewar Nash, though it's no substitute for the superlative 1930-32 Twin Ignition Eights and Ambassadors with their impeccable lines and proud radiators.

Announced in the improving economic climate of 1939 was a new Ford make that's with us still: Mercury, named for the speedy "messenger of the gods." The brainchild of company president Edsel Ford, it was Dearborn's first direct competitor to GM's B-O-P trio and the Dodge/DeSoto duo from Chrysler. Compared to that year's Ford, the first Merc was just a little larger, more powerful, and accordingly more expensive, and adwriters waxed poetic over its column-mounted gearlever. But it was a good seller. The market called for about 75,000 of

Left: *Cadillac offered convertible coupes in three series for 1939. Prices ranged from $1770 for a Series 61 with 135-bhp V-8, to a lofty $5440 for a V-16 Series 90.*

Two of Lincoln's ragtops for 1939: a Zephyr convertible coupe (above) with 110-bhp V-12; and a LeBaron-bodied Model K convertible sedan (below) with 150-bhp V-12. Prices were $1747 and $5828, respectively.

the '39s, divided among three sedans and a five-seat "convertible club coupe," a $1018 top-liner. Mercury volume would continue at this level through 1941.

Like main rivals Packard and Cadillac, Ford's luxury leader, Lincoln, cataloged a plethora of factory and custom bodies for its big L, K, KA, and KB chassis of 1930-35. This naturally included convertible coupes and sedans, mainly supplied by the likes of Brunn, Dietrich, and LeBaron. All were predictably scarce: in 1934, for example, just 25 Brunns, 45 LeBarons, and 25 Dietrichs were produced. As with Cadillac's Sixteen, the lush Lincoln K and its big V-12 would be built through 1940 in rapidly diminishing numbers, which made for individual open models as rare as any in this period.

Again like its rivals, Lincoln weathered hard times by fleeing to the medium-price field, but with a far more radical car: the 1936 Zephyr. Based on a rear-engine concept by John Tjaarda, it emerged with a conventional chassis but the most balanced streamlining yet seen from Detroit—far prettier than the Airflow's, for instance—a tribute to Edsel Ford and E.T. "Bob" Gregorie. It was also the first car in which aircraft-type stress analysis actually proved the advantage of unit construction. At 3300 pounds, the Zephyr was both lighter and stiffer than most comparable cars. Its powerplant, a 100-bhp L-head V-12 derived from Ford's flathead V-8, proved troublesome, but sales took off as Lincoln, like Packard, became a high-volume make for the first time in its history.

Two more convertibles from Ford for 1939: A first-year Mercury (top), and a Ford Deluxe (above). The Merc offered a 95-bhp V-8 for $1018; the Ford, an 85-bhp V-8 for $788. The Ford was quite popular, as 10,422 were produced.

Zephyr body styles initially comprised the expected coupe and sedan. Convertibles didn't appear until 1938, but they were worth the wait: two- and four-door models that benefitted from that year's effective facelift and longer wheelbase. The basically similar '39s were further improved via hydraulic brakes (belatedly adopted across the board in Dearborn) and a cooler-running V-12. Though worthy collectibles in their own right, these open Zephyrs led to an even more coveted convertible: the first-generation Continental, not in production until 1940, though the prototype built for Edsel Ford was based on a '39 Zephyr.

Less happy fates awaited one-time Lincoln foes Franklin and Pierce-Arrow, as well as Reo, a producer of excellent cars with singular styling. All went under well before the Forties dawned, not for lack of merit but as victims of the era's harsh economic realities.

Franklin, the nation's only successful builder of air-cooled cars, had always made money in the Twenties. But like many others, it greeted 1930 with more optimism and models than were justified, plus new styling and a new supercharged six with individually cast cylinders and overhead valves. Prices were cut to encourage sales of the similar 1931 models. It didn't work, but it was all they could do.

Franklin chassis were the basis for many custom bodies. One of the more unusual was the Pirate, a four-door convertible designed by Ray Dietrich, with concave lower-body contours that fully covered the runningboards—something everyone

Pontiac offered both six- and eight-cylinder convertible coupes for 1939. The Deluxe 120 came with an 85-bhp six and sold for $993. This Deluxe Eight (above) came with 100-bhp and sold for $1046.

would have 10 years hence. Dietrich also built four-passenger speedsters with foreshortened bodywork. Most were closed cars with permanent canvas-covered tops, but a full-convertible option was available at extra cost.

A convertible coupe was included in Franklin's new 1933 Olympic series, the firm's lowest-priced model line ever, cobbled up in a vain effort to stem mounting money losses. Powered by an L-head six *sans* supercharger, it was the product of a collaboration with Reo: basically a badge-engineered version of that outfit's latest Flying Cloud. At about $1500, the Olympic convertible was a good value, well built and pretty, but it was too little too late. Olympic production barely topped 1000 units for 1933-34; convertibles amounted to fewer than 100.

Reo, founded in 1904 by Ransom E. Olds (hence the acronym), never built more than 5000 cars a year after 1931. But several of them, particularly the convertibles, rank among the most classically beautiful automobiles ever created. Styling, by the talented Amos Northup, was always formal—based on the "correct" proportions, rooted in Greek

Left: *Lowest-priced Buick ragtop for 1939 was this Series 40 convertible coupe at $925.* Below: *Packard offered this 120 convertible sedan in 1939 for $1700.*

architecture, that distinguished the more memorable cars of the period. Straight eights powered a new 1931 Flying Cloud, offered on three different wheelbases; a still larger eight motivated the magnificent Royale, one of the earliest moves toward streamlining.

Inevitably, the Reo lineup was far too broad to sustain in the withering early-Thirties market. It was radically thinned by 1934 as the firm tried desperately to economize, though convertibles would persist for one more year. Still, the Flying Clouds, even the late shorter-wheelbase models, were truly beautiful, and the 135-inch-wheelbase Custom Eight convertible was as handsome a car as America built in these years. Reo

ceased car production in September 1936, though it survived as a truckmaker for another 40 years.

Convertible sedans and roadster-coupes were seen from Pierce-Arrow, another fine marque that died during the Depression. After several lean years, the firm regained its independence from Studebaker in 1933, emerging healthier than its erstwhile guardian. A new board of directors thought Pierce could break even at 3000 units a year and make a million dollars at 4000. But the respected stalwart built only 2152 cars through 1933, fewer than under Studebaker.

From there, it was all downhill despite the restyled, more streamlined 1934 models that paid homage to Phil Wright's daring '33 Silver Arrow show car. After little change for '35, the line was fully redesigned again, becoming more fashionably rounded still. Briefly, in 1936, it seemed Pierce had turned the corner, but sales soon tapered off again and production was suspended in 1937. A 1938 lineup was announced, but only 30 cars were registered by the end of that year.

Throughout this trying period, Pierce offered about as many open body styles as anyone. Among its 1934-35 Eights and 1936 models were "convertible roadster-coupes" seating just two passengers in utter glory on huge wheelbases. But production was the lowest imaginable. In 1937, for example, Pierce completed only 121 eight-cylinder cars in all, and just a handful were convertibles. That year's Twelves numbered only 71, with open styles totaling fewer than 10.

It is sad to recall the Depression's toll on such famous makes, if only because so many had distinguished histories and impressive cars. And the list goes on: Marmon, which never built a bad car and produced in its waning years of 1931-33 what many consider one of the best ever, the fabled Sixteen; Jordan, whose Playboy roadster had helped revolutionize car advertising; Peerless, another terminally ill veteran that sought to recover with a V-16, only to expire before it could reach production. All offered convertibles: Marmon its Eights and Sixteens (1930-33), Jordan its mid-range Eights (1930-31), Peerless its Standard and Master Eights (1930-31; only one Peerless Sixteen was built, a Murphy

sedan). A shame they had to die well before the Depression bottomed out.

But ironically, the automotive design developments of 1940-1975 would be almost wholly the result of lessons learned during the Thirties. If the Depression meant the end for some companies, it forced the survivors to think, plan, and invent. In so doing, they literally altered the shape of the automobile's future. Not until the fuel crises and market upheavals of the 1970s would American cars be so dramatically transformed.

Likewise, the Thirties saw open body styles change from "regular" models to the epitome of devil-may-care playfulness. One by one in 1929-30, then with a rush in 1931-34, the major manufacturers switched from old-fashioned roadsters and tourings to genuine convertibles—coupes and sedans with convenient folding tops and roll-up glass windows. Gradually, convertible top mechanisms acquired power assistance: hydraulic at first (as early as 1939), later electric. Meanwhile, the convertible coupe handily outgunned the costlier convertible sedan in popularity. By decade's end, only Hudson was building drop-top four-doors in any numbers.

The Thirties, then, was the era when the convertible acquired its modern image as a car for a limited but necessary market, designed as the ultimate sporty style among production bodies. Both trends would continue in the Forties, though they'd be interrupted by war and stalled a bit afterwards by an even more practical development: the *hardtop* convertible.

Cadillac offered convertible sedans in three series for 1939. This Series 75 Fleetwood is equipped with the optional "bustle-back" trunk.

THE CADILLAC·FLEETWOOD CONVERTIBLE SEDAN
{ with trunk }

The 1939 LaSalle Series 50 convertible coupe cost $1395 and came with a 322-cid V-8 producing 125-bhp. 1056 were built.

For the first time in years, Plymouth offered convertibles in both coupe (left) and sedan (above) body styles for 1939, but the latter would prove to be a one-year wonder; only 387 were built, Chrysler's last four-door convertible.

CHAPTER III

1940–49

A PERIOD OF REBUILDING

Left: *Top-of-the-line Series 90 Oldsmobile convertible coupe for 1940.* **Below left:** *1941 Plymouth Special Deluxe convertible coupe.*

Though most automotive highlights of the decade took place in the later years, much was accomplished at the beginning. As the economic climate improved, so did sales, and the auto industry began its recovery.

*J*ust as the Great Depression made an indelible mark on automotive history in the 1930s, World War II would do the same for the Forties, though having somewhat the opposite effect. While production (and for the most part, development) was curtailed during the war, the sellers market that followed spawned a host of fledgling automakers—however briefly. In the end, none of the newcomers survived, yet some promoted advancements reflected in later designs from the major manufacturers.

Though most automotive highlights of the decade took place in the later years, much was accomplished at the beginning. As the economic climate improved, so did sales, and the auto industry began its recovery. Despite (or maybe because of) the heightening war in Europe, 1940 saw nearly 3.3 million cars produced—a 50-percent increase over the previous year—even though defense contractors were siphoning off many skilled workers. Volume for 1941 was higher still, selling a record 4.3 million cars. But by the last day of 1941 the country had been at war three weeks, and civilian car production ended by government order two months later; it wouldn't resume for nearly four years.

Right: The 1940 Cadillac Series 62 convertible coupe was, at $1795, the company's least expensive ragtop. Only 200 were built.

This Century (left) was the lightest 1940 Buick convertible coupe to carry the company's larger, 141-bhp straight eight, yet only 550 were sold at $1343.

Historically, 1941 marks the beginning of the "standard-size" American car, the land cruiser that in a decade would be larger than anything built anywhere else in the world. In horsepower, from Willys to the heaviest Cadillacs, the trend was up. Chrysler products were redesigned and enlarged. Packard fielded the Clipper—longer, lower, and more streamlined than previous models. Studebakers were wider. Hudsons had longer wheelbases.

Convertibles sold well in a market swollen by the demands of a national economy revived by war work. About 160,000 were built in 1940-42—nearly 100,000 in 1941 alone, when soft-tops garnered a respectable 2.7-percent market share. Industry ranks had been sadly depleted, however. Big Three aside, the only automakers still around were independents American Bantam, Graham-Paige, Hudson, Hupp, Nash, Packard, Studebaker, and Willys-Overland.

Willys, then under the spirited leadership of saleswise Joe Frazer, launched a new 1940 line invoking patriotism, the Americar, but there were no convertibles. Ditto for Studebaker, Hupp, and G-P. The last two, barely alive, would leave the auto business after 1941.

American Bantam of Butler, Pennsylvania, would disappear too, but not before building its only convertible: the cute little Riviera. The Bantam had appeared in 1936 as an evolution of the American Austin (a license-built version of Britain's cheap and cheery Austin Seven) and was always offered as two-and/or four-passenger roadsters. The Riviera was more civilized and stylish, designed by Alex Tremulis (who'd go on to create the Tucker and many handsome designs for Kaiser-Frazer and Ford in the postwar period). Tremulis recalls that a Riviera would cruise at 75-80 miles an hour and average 42.5 miles per gallon—"but not at the same time!"

Forties Bantams were powered by a 20-horsepower, 50-cubic-inch four-cylinder engine (up from 13 bhp and 46 cid) in a simple chassis spanning a petite 75-inch wheelbase. The

Left: *Snappy 1940 Chevrolet cabriolet was available only in the top-line Special Deluxe series, but that didn't hurt sales; Chevy moved almost 12,000 of them.*

Riviera was the prettiest model, but Americans weren't quite ready for tiny cars of any kind and the firm was almost broke by 1939, when it built just 1229 vehicles. While turning out fewer than 1000 cars in 1940-41, Bantam sought salvation in the Army's new general-purpose-vehicle project, supplying the first acceptable prototype for what became the Jeep. It later turned entirely to building Jeeps, but the Army needed them faster than Bantam could deliver, and the firm went under once its contract was cancelled.

Before proceeding further, we should note that the convertible sedan disappeared from the American scene after 1942, not to return until Kaiser-Frazer's cobbled-up afterthought of 1949. Poor sales were obviously to blame: By 1941, entire industry production was less than 2000 units. Still, a few manufacturers (most notably within GM) still offered a line of "convertible phaetons," many quite memorable. Buick offered one in each of its five 1940 series, then deleted all but the Super and Roadmaster versions for '41 (though special-

Competing with Chevy's cabriolet was this 1940 Ford Deluxe convertible coupe. Though equipped with a V-8 (vs. Chevy's six), the Ford was slightly less popular with buyers.

order styles on the top-line Limited chassis were still cataloged, most executed by Brunn). Oldsmobile, meantime, belatedly fielded its first and only convertible sedans, both top-liners: a Series 90 for 1940 ($1570), a Custom Cruiser 8 (Series 98) for '41 ($1575).

LaSalle breathed its last in 1940, the only year when Cadillac's companion make offered two model lines. These were beautiful cars and somewhat scarce, none more than the ragtops. The junior Series 50 saw just 599 convertible coupes and 125 convertible sedans; respective figures for the plusher Series 52 Special were 425 and a mere 75. Cadillac then stepped up production of its Series 62 convertible sedan and priced it $230 below the 1940 version (of which only 75 were built). The result hardly seemed worth the effort, though: a paltry 400 for the entire 1941 model year.

America's only other late-prewar convertible sedans

Top right: This 1940 convertible sedan represents the last of the LaSalles. Only 200 were built. Right: 1940 Hudson Eight convertible coupe. Below: Lincoln Zephyr got a bigger V-12 (292-cid with 120-bhp) for 1940, but otherwise saw few changes.

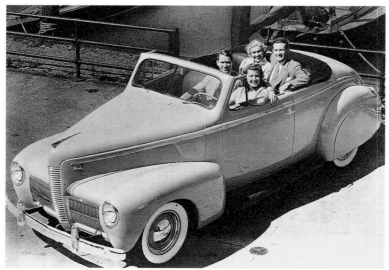

Right: *Nash offered cabriolets in each of its three series for 1940; Ambassador Eight, Ambassador Six, and the price-leading LaFayette.*

came from Mercury (1940) and Packard (1940-41). The 1940
Mercurys, which also included three closed sedans and a
convertible coupe, were lovely, with rounded, prow-front styling
by the talented Bob Gregorie. The Packards were far more
opulent; those with bodies designed by Howard A. "Dutch"
Darrin were possibly the most beautiful four-door convertibles
ever built.

Darrin's Packard connection stemmed from his 1937 decision
to return from Paris to Hollywood, where he set up a studio to
create exotic adaptations of production cars for movieland
society. His first such Packard was a convertible coupe on a
1938 Eight chassis for singer-actor Dick Powell; he did another
16-18 similar customs in 1938-39. With these, Dutch convinced
Packard to add three Darrins to its 1940 catalog: convertible
victoria (coupe), convertible sedan, and four-door sport sedan.

While Dutch had previously worked on the One Twenty
chassis, Packard insisted that these "production" Darrins be
Super Eights (Series One Eighty) for prestige reasons. The
sport sedan was quickly dropped, so most Darrin Packards
were convertible victorias. Only five '40s and one '41 were
convertible sedans, but they were the best of the lot. As Warren
Fitzgerald wrote, "They had the long 138-inch wheelbase,
combined with the three-inch longer hood, which made for
stunning proportions." Stunning prices, too: around $4600 for
the two-door, an imposing $6300 for the four-door.

Left: *By far the most expensive
Packard offered in 1940 was this
Darrin convertible sedan based on
the Custom Super Eight One Eighty
chassis. Few were sold at $6332.*

Right: 1941 Cadillac Series 62 convertible sedan. Below: Buick offered convertible sedans for 1941 in both the Super ($1555) and Roadmaster ($1775) series.

While the medium-priced One Twenty and Six had been essential during the Depression, they left the firm heavily oriented toward volume models. After the war, when it could have resumed building nothing but luxury cars, Packard continued down its prewar path and would ultimately be wiped out by Big Three competition.

But Packard's traditional place as America's luxury leader was in jeopardy by then. While the medium-priced One Twenty and Six had been essential during the Depression, they left the firm heavily oriented toward volume models. After the war, when it could have resumed building nothing but luxury cars, Packard continued down its prewar path and would ultimately be wiped out by Big Three competition.

The 1940-42 Packard lines abounded with convertible coupes and sedans, starting with the $1100 One Ten two-door. Though four-door converts were dropped after '41, two-doors were retained, as were their older, four-square bodies. The all-new '41 Clipper sedan, the first envelope-body Packard, met with great acclaim, but the war precluded a convertible derivative (though there would have been one otherwise by 1943).

Packard would get around to a Clipper-based ragtop, but not until the unfortunate "pregnant elephant" restyle of 1948. By that point, the lack of a convertible was so acutely felt that Packard released the Super Eight version six months before the rest of the line. Despite a shortish, 120-inch wheelbase, it was an impressive-looking car for the day, and relatively popular: 7763 were sold at $3250 each. Far more lavish was that year's Custom Eight ($4295), riding the 127-inch chassis and carefully crafted inside and out. Counting 1105 Custom Eights, Packard was the largest producer of luxury convertibles that year—for the first and last time after the war. From 1949 on, Cadillac's lone soft-top would outsell all of Packard's by four to one.

The only other convertibles from independent producers in 1940 were Nashes and Hudsons. All were fine examples of the two-door breed, with fresh, contemporary styling and hand-buffed leather upholstery. Confusingly, Hudson retained the term "convertible sedan" for its more lavishly equipped 1940 soft-tops and all its 1941-42s, though none had four doors. "Sedans" were identical in size and seating with convertible

Right: DeSoto offered only one ragtop for '41, this convertible coupe priced at $1240. Production ran to 2937 units.

Below: One of the most popular convertibles for 1941 was this Chevrolet Special Deluxe, of which 15,296 were sold at $949.

Above: "Subdued" aptly describes Chrysler styling for 1941, though the company offered a plaid, "Highlander" interior option to spruce up the inside.

Below: Ford adopted "busier" front styling for 1941, when the venerable flathead V-8 was joined by a new OHV six-cylinder—which cost $15 less.

coupes but cost more, partly because of detachable rear side windows that gave them a different top-up appearance (coupe tops had blind quarters). Both styles were available for 1940 as a DeLuxe Six, Super Six, and Eight.

Hudson's 1941 convertibles were engineered to be as solid and durable as its sedans (rare among period ragtops), with a specially designed, heavily reinforced frame for the first time. Hudson also offered its first power top, controlled by a dashboard button. Rear side windows were now standard but no longer detachable, lowering with the top instead. Offerings comprised Deluxe and Super Sixes and Commodore Six and Eight (the last three on 121-inch wheelbases, versus the Deluxe's 116). All continued for 1942.

Hudson produced about 1000 convertibles a year in 1940-41, far fewer in abbreviated model year '42. Unlike Packard, however, Hudson had planned well for convertibles and was thus able to offer them again immediately after the war, though choices were limited to Super Six and Commodore Eight.

Nash, like Hudson, had fully restyled for 1939. Its '40 facelift was similar, with a pointed nose carrying a slim vertical grille between chromed "catwalks" inboard of the headlamps. Nash switched to unit construction for 1941 but retained a separate body/chassis Ambassador convertible (called "All-Purpose cabriolet") in limited production for that year only. The model didn't surface again until 1948 when 1000 were built—Nash's last large ragtops.

From here on, the story is mainly one of convertible coupes. Surprisingly, the dominant convertible manufacturer by this time was not Ford or Chevrolet but Buick, which had long stressed open styles and usually sold a larger percentage than rival makes. For example, Buick built 18,569 of its '41 convertible two-doors—one model each in the Special, Super, and Roadmaster series—the highest count for any nameplate between 1937 and 1947. At just over $1000, the Special accounted for about half the annual totals. Buick had a banner '41 overall, producing 374,000 cars.

Right: *While Olds offered five convertibles for 1941, this top-of-the-line Custom Cruiser 8 was the only four door. Sadly, it would also be the last.*

Above: *The low-slung Continental became a separate model for 1941 rather than a Zephyr series. Price was cut slightly to $2865, while output reached 400 units.*

Right: *Next to the sleek Continental, Packard's One Twenty looked somewhat boxy by comparison—but at $1407, it cost only half as much.*

Like most everyone else, Buick warmed over its 1942 models as stopgaps for the first three years after the war, but the Special convertible and Century series didn't return. Relying strictly on $2000-$3000 Super and Roadmaster two-doors, Buick continued with the industry's highest convertible volume: 8600 in 1946, 40,000 in 1947, 30,000 in 1948. The big topless Roadmaster, with its huge chrome teeth and "gunsight" hood ornament, became a symbol of predicted peacetime prosperity, likely coveted by more Americans than anything else on wheels in 1946-47. Cadillacs, after all, were pricey; Buicks were more attainable.

Yet not all Forties Cadillacs were expensive. Once LaSalle departed, Cadillac spread down into the upper region of LaSalle's former price territory. One result was that a 1941-42 Sixty-Two convertible coupe could be had for under $2000. But perhaps people didn't realize this, because the ragtop didn't sell: Only 908 went out the door during 1940-42. Postwar, it was a different story: 1342 of the '46s, 6755 of the '47s. The Sixty-Two was the only Caddy convertible to survive the war, but then it was the only one needed.

In GM's mid-price ranks, Olds and Pontiac worked hard at selling their ragtops before the war, finding homes for 11,000 of their '41s combined. Neither make listed fewer than two

models, usually split between the top and bottom series. The Pontiacs cost about $1000; the '41 Oldsmobiles ranged from a $1048 six-cylinder 66 to the $1227 eight-cylinder 98 version. Both makes fielded similar offerings postwar, albeit at higher, inflation-fueled prices. The Olds 98 became one of GM's first new postwar cars with its mid-1948 "Futuramic" redesign. Convertible versions of both the "old" and the "new" 98s were available, and together they accounted for about three-fourths of the make's 1948 convertible sales, which totaled close to 17,000, making Olds number three in soft-tops behind Buick and Chevy. (Pontiac, at 16,000, ranked fourth.)

Chevy convertibles finally began outselling Ford's in 1940, when new "Royal Clipper" styling made for a thoroughly more attractive car than Chevy had built for some time. (Not inaccurately, some still describe it as a mini-Cadillac or Buick.) Chevrolet achieved this success with just one top-line convertible selling at $800-$1000 (a Special Deluxe for 1940-41, a Fleetmaster for 1942-48) and continued its lead after the war except in 1946. With its plodding "Stovebolt" six, a Chevy convertible couldn't keep pace with an open Ford V-8, but at least it looked better.

Ford and Mercury were restyled for 1941, but neither was an improvement and it showed: For the model year, Ford built

*Plymouth offered this striking
Special Deluxe convertible coupe
in 1941 for $1007. It proved quite
popular with buyers, as 10,545
were built.*

only 700,000 cars while Chevy topped the million mark for the first time. The advent of the Ford Six (equipped with a new overhead-valve inline six-cylinder engine) didn't help, though it was also offered as a convertible. Again like most others, both Dearborn makes relied on warmed-over '42s for 1946-48, but added luster to the lines with new limited-production convertibles: the wood-bodied Ford/Mercury Sportsmans.

Developed from Bob Gregorie's wartime styling sketches, the 1946-48 Ford and 1946 Mercury Sportsmans featured white ash and mahogany on doors, rear fenders and deck (structural around the aft quarters). It was an attractive way to freshen up the old styling, and it boosted showroom traffic. But the Sportsmans weren't cheap: $1982-$2282 for the Ford, $2209 for the Merc—about $500 upstream of their all-steel counterparts. Production thus ran to only 3487 Fords and just 205 Mercs. Glamorous convertibles were arguably best left to Lincoln.

And Lincoln's convertibles were glamorous indeed. Model year 1940 brought one of the decade's most stunning cars: the Zephyr-based Continental, an Edsel Ford idea executed by Bob Gregorie. Rakish long-hood/short-deck proportions, Dearborn's then-favored prow front, outside spare tire, and a sleek yet "formal" roofline made it "thoroughly continental" per Edsel's instructions. A closed coupe and wide-quarters cabriolet were offered at $2850 each, and they lured customers into dealerships by the thousands (some of whom went away in one of the less-expensive Zephyrs, which still included a shapely convertible two-door). The '41 Continental, split off from the Zephyr line, enjoyed slightly higher volume.

For 1942, all Lincolns acquired a more reliable, 305-cid version of the flathead Zephyr V-12, plus a flashy facelift with higher, squared-up fenders, reduced ride height, and chromier, more complex grillework. The last was revised for postwar

models, which were prewar carryovers except that the 292-cid engine returned and the "Zephyr" name didn't. The Continental reached a yearly production peak in 1947 at 1569 units, only to vanish a year later (though not permanently).

Chrysler Corporation's 1940-42 convertibles were conventional and low-key, sprinkled among the various lineups wherever it was thought they'd do the most good. Chrysler offered Windsor Six and New Yorker Eight models, the former occasionally sporting vivid "Highlander plaid" or "Navajo" upholstery. Dodge and Plymouth had one apiece, slotted into their higher-price spreads. Ditto DeSoto except for 1942, when it offered Custom and Deluxe ragtops. Appropriate, perhaps, since DeSotos were more interesting that year, bearing "Airfoil" hidden headlamps (the first since the Cord 810/812's) and a sculpted, half-dressed maiden as a new mascot. The eyelids vanished postwar, but the hood ornament persisted through '48.

One of the most memorable of all Chryslers surfaced in 1946: the wood-trimmed Town & Country, a sleek wagon prewar, now an elegant closed sedan and convertible coupe. The topless T&C, beloved of Hollywooders from Tyrone Power to Leo Carrillo, was the better seller and more successful than Ford's Sportsmans, with over 8500 built through early 1949.

The T&C's white ash trim was sheer hell to maintain, but this wasn't much of a problem for the new-car-every-year folks able to afford such rigs. Besides, it was one of the few really interesting cars in 1946-47. The last T&C ragtops of 1949 sold for over $3900, which was more than most Cadillacs, while all-steel Windsor and New Yorker convertibles soldiered on at $2000-$2500. While it lasted, the T&C was good publicity.

Led by upstart newcomer Kaiser-Frazer, Detroit's first all-new postwar designs began appearing in 1946, though because

Right: *Lincoln built 191 of its $2150 Zephyr convertible coupes for 1942. This was the only year that an enlarged, 305-cid V-12 with 130-bhp was offered.*

Dodge closed out its prewar production with this $1245 Custom convertible coupe (left). It cost nearly $200 more than its Chevy counterpart, but actually beat the Chevy in sales—by 3 units.

of an unprecedented seller's market, most would be held back until model year '49. K-F, of course, had it easy, having built no cars prewar and thus having no dies to amortize. Predictably, its initial entries were sedans (bearing smooth, slab-sided Dutch Darrin styling). Convertibles would have to wait.

This left Studebaker to release the industry's first new postwar soft-tops: the 1947 Regal Deluxe Champion ($1902) and Commander ($2236), of which 6000 were built by January 1948. The 112-inch-wheelbase Champion was on the stubby side, but the Commander looked very good indeed, a tribute to the radical new styling by Virgil Exner of the Raymond Loewy team.

Most other makes apparently considered convertible coupes important enough to include them as part of their new postwar fleets. Only Oldsmobile, Nash, and Kaiser-Frazer didn't have one, and each was a special case. K-F was new, but would shortly go topless. Nash elected to build no large convertibles after '48. Olds introduced its new-design postwar models in two stages: the 98 as a mid-1948 entry, the 76 and 88 as '49s—by which time each had a convertible, 98 included.

Hudson and Kaiser-Frazer built the most unorthodox early-postwar soft-tops. The former debuted its famous "Step-down" cars for 1948, with smooth, low lines and unitized construction of extraordinary strength. Among them were no fewer than three convertibles, more than any other manufacturer: Super Six and Commodore Six/Eight. Called "brougham" (thus reviving pre-1940 nomenclature), they bore a broad steel header above the windshield. Hudson claimed superior roll-over protection, but this was probably more a matter of economics; the header was simply a remnant of decapitating the closed two-door body to eliminate the need for separate convertible dies.

Kaiser-Frazer's convertible, announced for 1949, was unique for its day in having four doors. Production economies were

Left: *Mercury's V-8 got a power increase from 95- to 100-bhp for 1942. At $1215, it cost $125 more than Ford's 90-bhp Super Deluxe convertible coupe.*

Top: *DeSoto's only ragtop for 1946 was this convertible coupe in the Custom series. Though a virtual carryover from '42, it cost over $400 more at $1761.*

Above: *One step down on the Chrysler ladder was this 1946 Dodge Custom convertible coupe at $1649. A mild facelift differentiated it from the '42's.*

*Chevy brought back its ever-popular
Fleetmaster convertible coupe after
the war. Though the price had
jumped almost $400 (to $1476),
few seemed to mind.*

*Plymouth gave its Special Deluxe
convertible coupe a little sprucing
up for 1946, though at $1439, it
would probably have sold just as
well without it.*

at work here, too, because a four-door sedan was the only body style K-F had. Like Hudson's, its convertible's header was carved from a sedan roof, leaving a small but noticeable expanse of steel.

Unfortunately, the prototype K-F convertible lacked the structural integrity of Hudson ragtops. As engineer Ralph Isbrandt remembered: "It was like a bowl of jelly... You couldn't see out the rearview mirror on a smooth road. We finally convinced management that GM, Ford, and Chrysler weren't putting X-member frames and special pillars on convertibles for the fun of it, and then we began to get results... but the frames alone cost us $600 each. They were not only 'X'd' but reinforced all over hell. Every time we could find another patch we would slap it on."

When body engineer John Widman pointed out that the convertible needed structural B-pillars, stylist Buzz Grisinger came up with vertical glass panels framed in chromed metal to provide the necessary reinforcement without disrupting the body lines. It was a makeshift arrangement at best. Neither the little panes nor the chrome side-window frames were removable or retractable, remaining in place with the top up or down. It was all just a funny exercise, as only 124 of the '49s were called for: about 54 Kaisers and 70 Frazers. A handful were reserialed as 1950 models.

Ford and Chrysler entered 1949 with all-new designs across the board, and GM completed its postwar overhaul with like updates for Chevy, Pontiac, Buick, and the junior Oldsmobiles. (The Olds 98, as mentioned, and all Cadillacs save limos

Right: *Pontiac offered both a
Torpedo Six and Torpedo Eight
convertible coupe for '46. Prices
were $1631 and $1658, respectively.*

Opposite, top: One of the most collectible of all 1940s convertibles is the 1946 Chrysler Town & Country, with its real wood paneling. **Right:** *Pontiac's ragtops changed little for '47, but prices rose by about $200.*

Opposite, left center: Buick was Convertible King in '47 with 40,371 sales. Opposite, right center: 1947 Hudson Super Six. This page, center: Studebaker was "First by far with a postwar car" with its all-new '47 line.

Both Ford (opposite, bottom) and Mercury (below, right) offered wood-sided Sportsman convertible coupes in 1946, but only the Ford returned for '47. Ford sold 1209 in 1946, Mercury only 205. For '47 (pictured), Ford sold 2250.

were redesigned for '48.) Ford and GM adopted much sleeker lines on full-envelope bodies; Chrysler persisted with bolt-on rear fenders and a more upright stance.

GM's styling was arguably the best—inspired, according to design chief Harley Earl, by the wartime Lockheed P-38 pursuit fighter aircraft. Every make wore smooth, flowing bodywork and, Chevy excepted, distinctive hallmarks. Pontiac had "Silver Streaks," Buick "ventiports," Oldsmobile rocket insignia (denoting the division's new high-compression overhead-valve V-8), and Cadillac (which had its own new short-stroke V-8 that year) tailfins and massive eggcrate grilles.

Buick, once a cornucopia of convertibles, cancelled its Super but produced over 30,000 Special and Roadmaster models—massive, brightly decorated cars selling respectively for about

Right: Sporting the industry's first tailfins, this 1948 Series 62 convertible coupe was the only ragtop Cadillac offered that year. 5450 were sold at $3442.

Below: In direct competition with the drop-top Caddy was this 1948 Lincoln convertible coupe. Though less expensive ($3142), it sold far fewer copies.

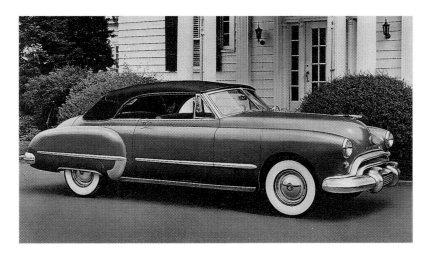

Lincoln ended the Continental Mark I series with this 1948 model. It looked similar to the standard Lincoln, but cost $4746; only 452 were built.

Oldsmobile debuted "Futuramic" styling on its 1948 Series 98 models—a year ahead of the rest of its line. 12,914 convertible coupes were sold at $2624.

$2100 and $3100 and riding 121/126-inch wheelbases. Chevy did even better with 32,932 examples of its sole convertible, in the Styleline Deluxe series, a neat little car still well liked today. Cadillac continued with its solitary Series 62 ragtop, of which 8000 were sold at $3442. Pontiac and Oldsmobile, spanning a broader price spread, cataloged five convertibles between them. Olds served up three, ranging from $2148 (in the six-cylinder 76 series, fast waning in sales) to $2973 (the big 98, the most popular at 12,602 units). The Pontiacs were all deluxe-trim models in the Chieftain Six and Eight series, tagged at around $2200.

But Ford had America's favorite 1949 convertible, wresting the sales lead from Chevy on the strength of its fine new postwar design by Dick Caleal of the George Walker organization. Offered only as Custom V-8, the soft-top accounted for 51,133 units, the highest of any Ford convertible yet. Lincoln and

Mercury were also rebodied for '49, becoming large, bulbous "bathtub" styles—distinctive if not exactly pretty (though arguably more so than Nash's similar attempt). Lincoln had two soft-tops, standard and Cosmopolitan, costing $3200/$4000 and produced sparingly: only 743 for the calendar year. Mercury's single entry, priced at a more attractive $2410, brought 16,765 sales, another record.

Had there been styling awards in '49, Chrysler Corporation would have received the "Most Underwhelming" trophy. As ever, this company was dominated by engineers, and the '49s proved it. Square and upright, they sold well only while the booming seller's market lasted.

Among Highland Park's '49 convertibles, Plymouth, Dodge, and DeSoto offered one each, in the higher-priced series as usual. Strong, and assembled with care using fine materials, they'd be remembered for their rust-resistance if nothing else.

The 1948 Ambassador convertible coupe was Nash's first postwar ragtop; it was also the last—at least of its full-sized models. 1000 were sold.

89

Above: *1948 Plymouth Special Deluxe convertible coupe; $1857.* Left: *1948 was the first year for Packard's "pregnant elephant" styling. Convertibles came in the Super Eight ($3250) and Custom Eight ($4295) series.*

Studebaker's most expensive car (and only ragtop) for 1948 was this Commander Regal Deluxe convertible coupe, priced at $2431.

Sales reflected the dowdy styling: the three makes combined managed just 6000 soft-tops. Plymouth did the best with 3110, but Ford and Chevrolet sold 10-15 times as many—an indicator of the narrowing Plymouth appeal that would lead to a crisis at Chrysler by 1954.

The firm's most interesting '49 convertibles again carried Chrysler nameplates. The Windsor Six and New Yorker Eight were back, accompanied by a handsome New Yorker-based Town & Country. There was less wood than before, but the T&C remained a singular automobile. Counting 1000 of these, Chrysler sold nearly 5000 of its '49 convertibles. Obviously, what few soft-top customers the company had tended to buy Chryslers.

Nineteen-fifty dawned with the industry loaded for bear. No fewer than 33 convertibles were offered that year, a new record. But the great postwar seller's market had nearly peaked. For Chrysler and the independents at least, retrenchment would too soon prove the order of the day.

The convertible was about to retrench too, thanks to a revolutionary 1949 development: the "hardtop convertible." The term came from GM, leading the way in styling innovations as usual—though Chrysler was nearly first with this one, having built seven prototype Town & Country hardtops in 1946, only to back away from production at the last minute.

No matter. The hardtop was an idea whose time had come: a convertible coupe with a roof that *didn't* convert. Alternatively, it could be thought of as a traditional closed coupe *sans* structural B-pillars. Either way, rolling down front and rear side windows made for a wide open space twixt top and beltline— and sportier looks than those of any pillared style. It also afforded much of the "airy" feel of convertibles combined with the superior rigidity, quietness, and convenience of a

Top left: *Automatic transmission was a new option for Pontiac in 1948, when Torpedo Six and Eight convertibles were offered at $2025 and $2072, respectively.*

Above: *"Unique" is perhaps the kindest word used to describe the 1949 Frazer Manhattan four-door convertible. At $3295, only about 70 were sold.*

Top right: *Buick redesigned its '49 line, the first to employ the famous "portholes." Dynaflow automatic was now an option on the Super series.*

Right: The big news at Cadillac for '49 was a new, more powerful OHV V-8 that put out 160-bhp. The only convertible offered, this Series 62 sold for $3442.

Chrysler restyled its cars for 1949, and once again offered a Town & Country convertible. Price was now up to a lofty $3970, and only 1000 were built.

fixed steel roof.

To be sure, the hardtop was a compromise, but that was its very appeal: the best of both worlds. It didn't take long to take off. By the mid-Fifties, the hardtop coupe, as some would call it, ranked second only to the mainstay four-door sedan as Detroit's most popular body style. Eventually it spawned four-door hardtop sedans and, in some model lines, even pillarless wagons.

It's thus instructive to record the hardtop's beginnings in 1949 with a trio of GM models: Buick Roadmaster Riviera, Cadillac Series 62 Coupe de Ville, and Oldsmobile 98 Holiday. All vied with corresponding convertibles as top of the line and were similarly trimmed, with leather upholstery and simulated chrome bows on headliners. Reflecting such finery, and perhaps the novelty of the idea, the Buick and Cadillac hardtops actually sold for a few dollars *more* than their ragtop sisters (the two Oldsmobiles cost the same). Production was

accordingly limited—4343 Rivieras, 2150 Coupe de Villes, 3006 Holidays—though these were mid-year introductions and thus in somewhat short supply. GM would correct both pricing and production in a big way for 1950.

We might also mention that the hardtop idea dates from at least the mid-Teens, seen in developments like coupes with removable center posts and, in the Twenties, the rigid accessory "Carson top" for roadsters. Then, as in 1949, buyers wanted sportier looks without giving up comfort and convenience. In the Fifties and Sixties, these same factors, together with increasingly unpleasant driving conditions and the advent of reliable, low-cost auto air conditioning, would further boost hardtop sales at the convertible's expense.

Still, those later years produced some of the greatest and most memorable of American convertibles. For their story you need only read on, beginning with the next chapter and the fabulous Fifties.

CHAPTER IV

1950–59

THE AGE OF
GLITTERY EXCESS

If any period can be said to have been the convertible's "golden age," the 10 years beginning with 1957 was it. An era of unabashed jukebox styling and ever-climbing horsepower, the Fifties saw the American car reach its zenith— unchallenged by and invulnerable to any foreigner.

1959 Cadillac Series 62 convertible coupe.

Over the course of the decade, wind-in-the-hair aficionados would have an ever-widening selection of convertibles from which to choose, despite the fact that the number of nameplates was shrinking. While the decade began with all the independents solvent and enjoying good production, it didn't end up that way. By 1960, Packard, K-F, and Willys were gone, Nash and Hudson had vanished into American Motors, and Studebaker was backing away from the abyss that had nearly swallowed it in 1958.

Of course, this had little or nothing to do with the convertibles they produced—or didn't produce—and everything to do with management. As General Motors' chairman Frederick Donner said in 1958 to a reporter mourning the sad straits of Studebaker-Packard: "Ask them what they did with their huge wartime profits. Did they plough them back into the business, as we did? We didn't drive them where they are. They did that on their own."

Still, the overall dominance achieved by GM and Ford in this decade is precisely mirrored in convertible production.

With one exception—1951, when Plymouth ranked fourth—Detroit's ragtop volume leaders were Ford, Chevrolet, Buick, Olds, and Pontiac.

And we're talking about really serious numbers of convertibles for the first time. Though output peaked in 1957 at over 300,000, the best year on a percentage basis was—believe it or not—recession-year 1958, when soft-tops grabbed an unusually high five-percent market share.

Then too, as the independents failed or faltered, the Big Three moved to take their place, fielding more models and sub-models spanning ever-wider market sectors. Convertibles were naturally among them. Thus Ford Division, for example, which for years had gotten by with only one or two convertibles in the line, left the Fifties with three—and would have eight by 1966. If any period can be said to have been the convertible's "golden age," the 10 years beginning with 1957 was it.

An era of unabashed jukebox styling and ever-climbing horsepower, the Fifties saw the American car reach its zenith—unchallenged by and, through 1956, apparently

For 1950, Dodge added roll-up windows (in place of side curtains) to the winsome Wayfarer (above), transforming it from a "roadster" into a true convertible. The price remained the same at $1727.

Only minor detail changes were made to the Mercury line for 1950. Price of the convertible went up a whopping $2 to $2412, yet production was only half that of 1949, at 8341 units.

Little changed for 1950; Pontiac still offered both six- and eight-cylinder convertibles on the same 120-inch wheelbase. Shown (above) is the Chieftain Eight Deluxe, with a 108-bhp straight eight, priced at $2190—only $68 more than the six.

invulnerable to any foreigner. Production went nowhere but up in the rising affluence of the Eisenhower years, setting record after record. For Americans at least, Detroit was king and all was right with the world.

Historically, the decade splits neatly in half: 1950-54, when most makers continued to update their initial postwar designs; and 1955-59, when higher horsepower and radical restyles were typically annual developments. Each period had one definite "check" year: 1952, when the Korean War curtailed civilian auto production; and 1958, when a recession cut deeply into car sales, giving imports their first firm toehold in the U.S. market and prompting domestic compacts to compete.

By 1950, nearly every manufacturer had introduced a new postwar design. But Ford was perhaps a step ahead of most other major makes, with smooth-sided styling that did away with any hint of separate rear fenders. This advanced design (along with V-8 availability) made Ford the drop-top king in the early part of the decade, typically outselling rival Chevy nearly two to one. In fact, Ford remained the leader in convertible production for eight of these 10 years, 1950-57, while building some of the most radical topless models we'd ever see. Its approach through 1954 was straightforward: a single high-line soft-top. All 1950-51 Fords were improved versions of the all-new make-or-break '49 design, with the convertible continuing in the upper-level Custom series. A chunky, well built car on a 114-inch wheelbase, it was one of the few Fords available only with V-8. Ford was on to

Hudson convertibles of this period had a heavy "brow" over the windshield – a remnant of the top that was chopped off. Shown at left is a 1950 Commodore 8.

something here. The convertible's image demanded more than a six-cylinder could deliver, so Ford's soft-top had a huge advantage over the "stovebolt-only" Chevy. Plymouth wisely paid heed and went the same route beginning with its '55 convertible.

Ford stole a big march on Chevy (which wouldn't be redesigned until '55) with its all-new '52, a fine piece of work by Frank Hershey, George Walker, and others. Though lower and smoother, boxy lines made it look otherwise despite an inch-longer wheelbase. The lineup expanded to three series. The convertible, newly designated Sunliner, was in the top Crestline group, still with standard V-8. Base price was just over $2000. The Sunliner remained in this position through the extensive restyle of 1955-56, when it became part of the new top-line Fairlane series, named for Henry Ford's estate. By that point, Ford was offering a second convertible—and with only two seats: the Thunderbird.

Ordained by division general manager Lewis Crusoe and styled by Bill Boyer under Hershey's direction, the T-Bird was Ford's better mousetrap. Dearborn had looked hard at Chevrolet's 1953-54 Corvette and found it wanting. The

Chevy's convertibles were out-sold (probably because they were out-performed) by Ford's ragtops in the early Fifties. This 1951 Chevy DeLuxe Styleline (right) was priced at $2030; 20,172 were sold.

Despite rising prices, sales of Cadillac's ragtop remained strong. This Series 62 convertible coupe (right) cost $3987 in 1951, when 6117 were sold.

Hudson debuted the famed Hornet in 1951, with its 308-cid, 145-bhp straight six. Shown (left) in $3099 convertible form, the Hornet became a formidable racer.

*Mercury charged $2380 for its
1951 convertible (below), and
sold 6759 of them. All Mercs
received new rear-end styling
that year.* **Bottom:** *Prototype
for 1951 Kaiser convertible.
Sadly, it was never produced.*

Thunderbird would show what a two-seater should be. Ford made it a genuine convertible with roll-down windows and gave it a bolt-on hardtop for wintertime comfort (Corvette acquired these for '56). The 'Vette body was fiberglass, the T-Bird's conventional steel. Early Corvettes had six-cylinder engines; the T-Bird bowed with a burly Mercury V-8, part of the new overhead-valve family that first appeared in Fords for '54. Also unlike the early Corvettes, manual transmissions were available. The Bird did race, but it was really a "boulevard sports car."

The concept worked: For debut '55, Ford's two-seater outsold Chevy's 24:1. But the rivalry ended almost as soon as it began. Corvette was transformed into a genuine sports car—and a convertible—for '56, while the Thunderbird became a four-seater—and a hardtop—after 1957. But the convertible remained, accounting for one of every seven T-Birds sold in 1959.

If the Thunderbird was romantic, Ford's 1957-59 retractable-hardtop Skyliner was exotic. Employing a feature proposed for the Mark II Continental, it was the only mass-market

Odd little 1951 Nash Rambler Custom convertible coupe featured a unique "roll back" top. Priced at $1993, it was actually about $45 more than a Ford convertible.

convertible of its kind (though not the first: Peugeot had one in its 1936 Eclipse, and Chrysler's 1940 Thunderbolt show car was a "retrac" too). It seemed like a good idea at the time, and Ford made a legitimate point by asking, "How can it be a 'hardtop *convertible*' if the top doesn't go down?" But as a typically Fifties idea, the Skyliner proved a complicated beast with lots to go wrong.

Sharing Ford's all-new '57 platform, the biggest ever, the Skyliner had a huge steel roof that disappeared into a high, wide rear deck via a bevy of servo motors and miles of wiring. Even then, the top had to have a hinged front flap to fit, and left precious little trunk space when stowed. The "retrac" was expensive, too: over $400 more than the soft-top Sunliner (both offered only in top-line Fairlane 500 trim). That combined with mechanical problems to turn off customers, and production went from 20,766 for model year '57 to 14,713 for '58, then to 12,915 for '59, after which the Skyliner was abandoned (at the bidding of division chief Robert S. McNamara) as a superfluous gimmick.

Certainly one of 1950's best-looking convertibles, this Oldsmobile Futuramic 88 (above) carried the firm's 135-bhp V-8 in the lighter of two body styles. Price was $2294.

Packards received new styling for 1951 (right), but many thought they looked little better than their bulbous predecessors. Only one convertible was now offered, at $3391.

104

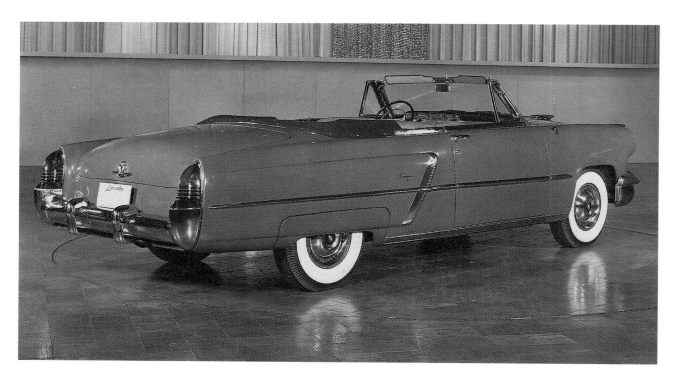

Opposite, top: *Buick offered ragtops in each of its three series for 1952. Shown is the top-line Roadmaster.* **Opposite, middle:** *1952 Hudson Wasp carried a 127-bhp straight six.* **Opposite, bottom:** *All-new 1952 Lincoln Capri; $3665, 1191 built.* **Above:** *The Mercury line was also restyled for '52. Pictured is the Monterey convertible, priced at $2370.*

Other unique retrac features included a V-8 as standard (extra-cost on Sunliners from '55), relocated fuel tank (behind the back seat instead of under the trunk floor) and foreshortened greenhouse. Like other Fords, the Skyliner was heavily restyled and re-engineered for 1959. At mid-year it became part of the new top-line Galaxie series, though it still wore Fairlane 500 script. More fascinating than ever today, the Skyliner remains a monument to a time when Detroit thought it could do anything.

Mercury had nothing so radical, and no two-seat sports cars, but convertibles played a role in its Fifties fortunes. For 1952 it reverted from 1949-51's "small Lincoln" to its original status as a "big Ford." It reached peak sales in 1955-57 with over 10,000 soft-tops a year, making it seventh in convertibles after Ford and the five GM divisions. There was only one Mercury convertible through mid-decade, always in the most expensive series (Monterey for 1952-54, Montclair for '55). Beginning with the '56s, certain Mercury hardtops were called "Phaetons," though they were nothing of the sort.

That same year, Mercury began moving into Ford country with the low-price Medalist series and added a less costly convertible to the step-up Custom line, priced at $2712 (versus $2900 for the soft-top Montclair). Mid-model-year '57 brought a third convertible, a roofless version of the glitzy Turnpike Cruiser.

Billed as a "dramatic expression of dream car design," the Turnpike Cruiser was conceived mainly as a top-line hardtop coupe and sedan. Both shared 1957's new Mercury-only body/ chassis and jazzy styling, but stood apart with "skylight dual curve" windshield, reverse-slant roofline with drop-down backlight, dual air intakes atop the A-pillars (housing little radio antennae no less), and "Seat-O-Matic," an embryonic memory seat that assumed one of 49 preset positions at the twist of a dial. Only the last was found on the Convertible Cruiser, which arrived as a replica (complete with owner-applied decals) of the one that paced that year's Indianapolis 500.

Despite a raft of gimmicks including push-button Merc-O-Matic transmission—or perhaps because of them—only about 16,000 of the '57 Cruisers were built, of which 1265 were convertibles. The soft-top vanished for 1958, when Turnpike Cruiser applied only to hardtops in a Montclair sub-series. The name was then consigned to the scrap heap as Mercury reverted to a three-series line with two convertibles; base Monterey and top-echelon Park Lane.

For 1952, Pontiac stood pat and continued to offer two convertibles; a six and an eight. Still perched on the same 120-inch wheelbase and sporting only mildly facelifted '49 styling, the Chieftain Six sold for $2444, while the Eight was $2518.

Alfred Sloan's dictum of "a GM car for every price and pocketbook," was now turning into "a Buick, Olds, and Pontiac for every price" as the three divisions went toe-to-toe, model-for-model. This would prove disastrous in the very long run: In the Fifties, though, such intramural rivalries helped move a lot of cars.

Lincoln's more dignified clients were habitually offered one convertible through the Fifties. The big, bulbous 1950-51 Cosmopolitans, with their curious "sad-eye" faces, saw very few copies (536 and 837, respectively). Cosmo was demoted to junior status for '52 and Capri came in to head the line, the ragtop available only in the upper series. Convertible Capris saw somewhat higher volume than Cosmos but were no match for Cadillac, which typically sold about four times as many convertibles as Lincoln during this period. Capri then moved down to make room for Premiere as the premium version of the wildly restyled, longer-lower-wider 1956 design; again, the convertible stayed in the senior series. Lincoln sold 2447 soft-tops that year and 3676 of the '57s, the latter a record for the decade.

With dreams of rivaling GM as a multi-division producer, Ford formed a separate Continental Division to sell the $10,000 Mark II hardtop of 1956-57, then decided its impressive ultra-luxury car cost too much to build for what it brought in corporate prestige and showroom traffic. When Lincoln switched to a huge all-new unibody design for 1958, four Mark III derivatives were fielded as top-line models, though at much lower prices than the Mark II. Lincoln's convertible transferred to this line and sold at $6283; only 3048 were built. For 1959, Continental was folded back into a reconstituted Lincoln-Mercury Division and officially became a Lincoln again. That year's $7056 Mark IV convertible saw but 2195 copies.

1953 Buick Super

Buick, Olds, and Cadillac all produced "specialty" convertibles in 1953. **Above:** *The Buick Skylark was the most popular; 1690 were sold at $5000 each. Cadillac's Eldorado* (**right**) *cost a whopping $7750, yet sold 532 copies.*

Lincoln's best Fifties convertibles undoubtedly came in the 1952-54 "Road Race" years, when Lincoln built some of America's most roadworthy cars and dominated the Mexican Road Races. These Lincolns also happened to be gracefully styled and beautifully put together. Then Lincoln went wild with tailfins, slant-eyed fronts, and the "extruded look," losing quality as well as good taste. But that seemed to be exactly what the public wanted: 1957 and '58 were Lincoln's best convertible years.

Which brings us to Edsel, Ford Motor Company's ill-starred attempt at a second medium-price make. Though the very name has since become synonymous with "loser," Edsel wasn't nearly the failure people imagine it was. It cost Ford anywhere from $100 to $250 million—not exactly a drop in the bucket even for a big company, but no occasion for bankruptcy either—and it was not entirely unsalable: 50,000 units wasn't bad in recession '58, Edsel's first model year.

Granted, Ford had planned for much more, invested heavily in plant and dealerships, and initially fielded no fewer than four Edsel series on three different wheelbases. There were two convertibles: the $3200 Pacer, a close cousin to that year's Ford, riding a 118-inch wheelbase; and the $4000 Citation, a Mercury relative on a 124-inch chassis. Both had gadgets galore, like "Teletouch" automatic transmission controlled by

Left: *The "normal" Cadillac convertible for '53 was this Series 62. Equipped with a 210-bhp V-8, 8367 were sold at a more reasonable $4144.*

Below: *At the opposite end of GM's 1953 price ladder was Chevrolet, though this Bel Air convertible was Chevy's "top-line" model, priced at $2175.*

Dodge styling took a giant leap forward in 1953 (right), as did performance, courtesy of the division's first V-8; the 241-cid "Red Ram," with 140-bhp.

push buttons buried in the steering wheel hub, a surprisingly poor location. The Citation carried a jumbo 410-cid V-8 with 345 horsepower and was quite impressive at its price. But Edsel convertible output was ridiculously low: 1876 Pacers, 930 Citations.

The 1959 Edsel line was drastically trimmed and all models made more like Fords. There was only one convertible, in the upper-series Corsair group, on a middling 120-inch wheelbase; 1343 were built. Edsel died soon after the '60 models were announced. Again there was but one ragtop, in the remnant Ranger series. Production was a mere 76. The Edsel name was considered for the uplevel Ford Falcon compact that became the Mercury Comet, but had already become the butt of too many jokes. The automotive namesake of Henry Ford's

Chrysler was accused of offering rather dowdy styling in the early '50s, but you wouldn't know it by looking at this 1953 DeSoto Firedome convertible (left).

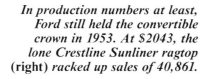

In production numbers at least, Ford still held the convertible crown in 1953. At $2043, the lone Crestline Sunliner ragtop (right) *racked up sales of 40,861.*

Right: *Having its convertible pace that year's Indy 500 certainly didn't hurt Ford sales in 1953.*

116

brilliant son deserved a better fate. (At least the name may gain a more positive image now that Edsel Ford II, son of late company chairman Henry Ford II, has been named to the Dearborn board of directors.)

Though Ford Division was the dominant make in Fifties convertible sales, General Motors was the decade's big gun in corporate convertible volume. Four of its brands—Chevrolet and the B-O-P nameplates—usually ran 2-5, and even Cadillac was no slouch, averaging about 10,000 topless cars a year.   ▷

Below: *Least successful of GM's "custom" convertibles in '53 was Oldsmobile's Fiesta. At $5717, it sold but 458 examples. Fiesta did not return for '54.*

Despite GM's flood of prestige convertibles in 1953, Packard still managed to sell 750 Caribbeans and 1518 of its "standard" convertibles

Pontiacs finally received a (very) mild styling update for 1953, most notably in the form of tiny fins added to the rear fenders (**right**).

Left: *At $2220, this snappy '53 Plymouth Cranbrook sold 6301 copies.* **Below:** *In answer to GM's specialty ragtops for 1953, Packard introduced the Caribbean, a lavishly endowed convertible selling for $5210.*

Buick adopted more modern, slab-sided styling for 1954, with convertibles being offered in each of four series. At right is the $2964 Super.

The Buick Skylark returned for 1954 (below), but was far less radical than its predecessor. It was also less expensive at $4483, yet only 836 were built.

Cadillac built some of GM's most interesting (and certainly most expensive) Fifties convertibles. Through 1952, the division continued with a single Series 62 model that tallied about 6500 units a year. For 1953, Cadillac added the Motorama-inspired Eldorado, essentially a 62 with custom interior, cut-down "Panoramic" wrapped windshield, distinctive notched beltline, and a metal instead of canvas cover for the stowed top. The Eldo wasn't intended to make a profit—and at $7750 and only 532 units, the '53 didn't—but rather to bring in customers for the ordinary models, which it did.

But when Cadillac restyled for '54, the game plan changed. Cut $2000 in price, the Eldorado went all out for sales: 2150 found buyers that year, thus establishing the model as a limited-production money-spinner. By 1955, Eldorados wore their own special "shark-fin" rear fenderlines; a year later came an Eldorado Seville hardtop to match the convertible, now called Biarritz.

Eldorados were technically part of the Series 62 until 1959, when they were broken out as a separate group. Combined, the Eldo and Series 62 put Cadillac convertible volume into five figures for the first time in 1955, a level that was usually maintained in subsequent years. The Eldo was heroically overdecorated next to the 62, glistening with chrome and $2000 dearer. But though never intended for high volume, it did account for up to 20 percent of Cadillac's convertible

Cadillacs became longer, lower, and wider for 1954. The Eldorado (above) returned, though it more closely resembled the Series 62 ragtop than did the previous year's "special." Price was cut to only $4538, and 2150 were sold.

Dodge paced the Indy 500 in 1954, and produced 701 "replica" convertibles based on the new Royal V8 series. Known as the Royal 500, all came with Dodge's "Red Ram" V-8 that produced 150-bhp from 241-cid.

Left: *Nash debuted the tiny, two-seat Metropolitan for 1954, long before anyone had ever heard the term "gas crisis." Convertibles sold for a paltry $1469.*

Left: *Packard continued its convertible for 1954, but sales were few—only 863. This would prove to be the final year for the "standard" Packard ragtop.*

Below: *1954 would also see the last Hudson Hornet convertible, with arguably the best styling of the "Step-down" period.*

production—quite good, all things considered.

In convertibles as most other matters, Cadillac outdid Lincoln as well as Packard, once a rival to both makes but fated to a sad death in the Fifties. Until the 1952 arrival of James Nance as company president, Packard had built convertibles almost as afterthoughts: a handful of dumpy Supers and Customs in 1950, then a series of short-wheelbase 250s on the junior (Clipper) body for 1951-53. The latter were nice, well built and reliable—and utterly boring. At $3400-$3500, they were more competitive with Buick and Chrysler than Cadillac.

Setting out to recapture past glories, Nance asked stylist Dick Teague to create a limited-edition soft-top for 1953. The result was the Caribbean, with handsome, clean-limbed open-wheel styling and a 180-bhp straight eight. At $5210, it was $2500 cheaper than the Eldo and thus handily outsold it. But Packard hit the skids in 1954, planning to bring out a new line but settling for a facelift. Only 400 of the '54 Caribbeans and 863 conventional convertibles were sold, all still with the junior body on its relatively short chassis.

But Nance got his big restyle for '55, including a lavish new Caribbean on the long wheelbase at last. It was Packard's only soft-top that year, priced at $6100. Historians say it was another traffic-builder never intended to make money, though it's hard to imagine Jim Nance okaying anything without profits in mind.

Packard had a fair year in 1955 but fell apart in 1956. Customers deserted what they perceived was a failing brand and dealers bailed out in favor of Big Three franchises while the factory nursed quality control and production problems. The '56 Caribbean was a fabulous car, and its reversible seat cushion covers (leather on one side, cloth the other) were a novel touch, but just 276 were built. Even then, there were leftovers.

Above: *New, slab-sided styling was adopted by Oldsmobile for 1954. With its 185-bhp V-8, this Starfire was the most expensive car in the line at $3249.*

*"Customized" Packard Caribbean
(top), returned for 1954, but
the price jumped to $6100; 400
were built. Above: 1955 Cadillac
Series 62 received a 250-bhp
version of the 331-cid V-8.
8150 were sold at $4448.*

Packard hastened its decline by purchasing Studebaker in 1954, which turned out to be a losing proposition. Having absorbed most of Packard's remaining capital and good will, Studebaker became the dominant partner, and the 1957-58 Packards were just glorified Studebakers. We can be glad there were no convertibles among them—and sad for the end of a great marque.

Returning to General Motors, we find a vast range of convertibles in the popular Buick, Olds, and Pontiac lines spanning the wide medium-price sector of the Fifties market. But Alfred Sloan's dictum of "a GM car for every price and pocketbook," was now turning into "a Buick, Olds, and Pontiac for every price" as the three divisions went toe-to-toe, model-for-model. This would prove disastrous in the very long run: a quarter-century later, GM was saddled with multi-make dealerships selling near-identical model groups to increasingly bewildered buyers. In the Fifties, though, such intramural rivalries helped move a lot of cars.

Above: *The only Convertible offered by Plymouth in '54 was this Belvedere, at $2301.* **Right:** *Chevrolet shocked the marketplace when it introduced the all-new '55s, which boasted both clean lines and the "small block" V-8.*

Buick, usually the industry's leading convertible maker in the Forties, fell behind in the Fifties as Ford and Chevy volume soared. But Buick continued to place great emphasis on soft-tops. It began the decade with three, reviving a Super to complement Special and Roadmaster models, then wowed the public in 1953 with the handsome Skylark, a sort of Buick Eldorado.

The Skylark was the most successful of 1953's three limited-edition GM convertibles, seeing 1690 units compared to only 532 Eldorados and 458 Olds Fiestas. Another Harley Earl exercise, it sported a restyled lower body with full-radius rear wheel openings, and came with every conceivable extra:

whitewalls, power steering and brakes, station-seeker radio, and deluxe interior. The price was equally lush: $5000. Much cleaner than the chromey standard Buicks, the Skylark was bereft of their trademark fender portholes and used wire wheels instead of wheel covers. But its '54 successor was more conventional and—with big, tack-on chrome tailfins—rather gaudy. After only 836 of these, the Skylark was retired.

No matter. Buick was destined for bigger things—notably a production surge that would take it ahead of Plymouth into third place behind Chevrolet and Ford. This was achieved in calendar year '54 and model year 1955. Reflecting its exuberance, Buick offered no fewer than five 1954 convertibles:

Chrysler products also got new styling for '55. Above: The DeSoto Fireflyte packed a V-8 with 200-bhp, while the similar Chrysler Windsor (right) had "only" 188.

*Though DeSoto had some of its best sales years
in the Fifties, its place in the Highland Park
hierarchy was being steadily undermined by Dodge
from below and Chrysler from above. DeSoto
enjoyed record volume in 1955, almost outproduced
Chrysler in '57 — and was history by late 1960.*

*Dodge came up with some unusual
two-tone paint schemes for its
redesigned '55s (above).
That year also saw the debut of the
classic Ford Thunderbird (left).*

the aforementioned Skylark, the usual Special/Super/ Roadmaster trio, and one in the newly revived Century series. Prices ranged from the $2563 for the Special to $3521 for the Roadmaster. Arguably most desirable was the hot-rod $2963 Century, with the big 200-horsepower 322-cubic-inch Roadmaster V-8 in the lighter, short-wheelbase Special body. A well-tuned Century ragtop could do 0-60 mph in 10 seconds and 110 mph flat out. No wonder Buick sold about 5000 a year in 1955-57 at prices in the $3000-$3600 range.

A revised '58 Buick lineup saw the Super series trimmed and a new Limited version of the Roadmaster, priced $500 higher. Buick retained four convertibles (a Limited model replaced the previous Super), but these garish cruisers were

the wrong cars for a recession year. Suddenly, a public that seemed tired of the horsepower race and acres of chrome began turning to compact Ramblers and the strange little Volkswagen. The '59 Buicks were locked up before that became apparent, but were much better cars nevertheless: smooth if flamboyant, and well engineered. They were also renamed, with convertibles in the LeSabre, Invicta, and Electra 225 series at base prices of $3200-$4200.

Oldsmobile followed a more modest convertible program, fielding a 98 and Super 88 (plain 88 for '50) through 1956 (plus 973 tail-end 76 convertibles in 1950). The aforementioned '53 Fiesta, a semi-show car in the 98 line, was priced too high to sell ($5717) and vanished after just one year.

Left: *All-new for 1955, this top-of-the-line Montclair convertible coupe sported a 198-bhp V-8, by far the most powerful engine Mercury had ever offered. Starting at $2712, it sold 10,668 copies.*

After zooming to fourth in the industry by 1955, Olds confidently launched a restyled line of 1957 "Golden Rockets" that included 88, Super 88, and 98 convertibles. All continued through 1959 and notched combined output of up to 22,000 a year.

Pontiac, too, was far more flush by mid-decade, moving from its traditional sixth to the number five slot. Through 1953 it cataloged two soft-tops: a Six and Eight on identical wheelbases. The Six finished up in '54 and a new straight-eight Star Chief series arrived with that year's only Pontiac convertible. Though a ragtop was finally added to the baseline Chieftain series for 1958, it paled by comparison to the mid-'57 introduction of the fast and flashy Bonneville.   ▷

The Starfire (top) *and Super 88* (above) *were the only convertible models Oldsmobile offered in 1955, yet the two garnered sales of 9149 and 9007, respectively. Both carried a 324-cid V-8 producing 202 bhp.*

Above: *The Caribbean was the only convertible Packard offered for 1955. Though handsomely restyled and priced slightly lower, it sold only 500 copies.*

Above: *Pontiac got modern, slab-sided styling for 1955, as well as a new, 180-bhp V-8. The only convertible was offered in the top-line Star Chief series.*

Like Chevrolet, Plymouth also got fresh styling and a V-8 for 1955 — with up to 177-bhp. The Belvedere V8 convertible (left), sold for $2351.

Against V-8 Fords, Chevrolet had always had an uphill battle for convertible sales. As noted, its 1950-54 line of good-looking but low-powered six-cylinder cars never approached Ford's volume. But things began to change with the '55s: the best Chevys yet and, as many agree, some of the best American cars ever built.

Left column, top: *1956 Plymouth Belvedere; $2478.* **Left, middle:** *1956 Cadillac Eldorado sported distinctive fins.* **Left, bottom:** *1956 Buick Super; $3544.* **Above:** *1956 El Morocco was a Chevy with Cadillac-like fins grafted on.*

When Semon E. "Bunkie" Knudsen became Pontiac general manager in 1956, he set out to alter the make's rather staid image. Enter the Bonneville. Available only as a fully decked-out convertible, it was equipped with a fuel-injected, 347-cid version of the modern V-8 introduced by the company in 1955. It made for the fastest Pontiac yet—faster still with optional Tri-Power (three two-barrel carbs), able to leap the quarter-mile in 16.8 seconds. Nevertheless, a near-$6000 price made for only 630 sales that first year. The Bonneville was continued in the newly-styled '58 line, but a two-door hardtop was added

and prices were greatly reduced. At a more palatable $3586, convertible sales reached 3096. For 1959, still sharing bodyshells with Chevrolet but with its own distinctive styling, Pontiac made Bonneville its new top-line series, adding a wagon and hardtop sedan to the previous convertible and hardtop coupe. The drop-top sold over 11,000 copies.

Against V-8 Fords, Chevrolet had always had an uphill battle for convertible sales. As noted, its 1950-54 line of good-looking but low-powered six-cylinder cars never approached Ford's volume. But things began to change with the '55s: ▷

The 1956 Chevrolet Bel Air (right).
*Wasting no time in joining the
horsepower race, Chevy boosted
its optional V-8 up to 225-bhp.*

*For 1956, Mercury offered two
convertibles, one in the Custom
series at $2712 (shown above),
the other in the top-line
Montclair series for $2900.*

Lincoln Premier (left) got restyled for 1956, and was powered by a larger V-8 with 285-bhp. The convertible sold 2447 copies at $4747.

Pontiac offered only mildly facelifted styling for 1956, but the top-line Star Chief (above) sported a more powerful, 227-bhp V-8 as well as Pontiac's only convertible.

Buick Super convertible (below) *got sleeker styling for 1957, in addition to a brawnier, 300-bhp V-8. 2065 were built, selling for $3981 each.*

A price of $7286 made the 1957 Cadillac Eldorado Biarritz convertible (below) *an attractive deal to 1800 buyers. All Eldorados got a 325-bhp V-8.*

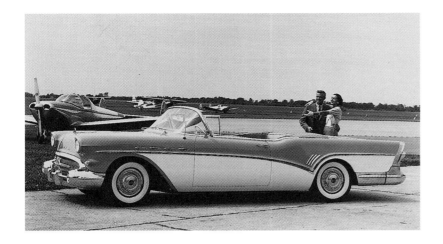

One of the most powerful cars of its day was the legendary 1957 Chrysler 300C (above). *It carried Chrysler's new "Forward look"— along with up to 390-bhp.*

Also displaying Chrysler's sleek '57 styling was this DeSoto Firedome convertible (above), *though it has somewhat tame by comparison, with "only" 230-bhp.*

the best Chevys yet and, as many agree, some of the best American cars ever built. They also ushered in Chevy's first modern V-8, the excellent 265 small-block, shepherded into production by chief engineer Ed Cole.

Suddenly, "Chevrolet" meant "performance," and a Bel Air convertible was the hottest low-price car around. No surprise, as the '55 Ford was a heavily facelifted '54, while the '55 Chevy was all-new, beautifully styled, built with care, and available in a raft of colors (including handsome two-tones). It only got better through the deft Cadillac-like restyles of 1956 and '57. We can see how this high-powered soft-top—transformed for '58 into an even more deluxe Impala model—altered the score by looking at some of the model year production figures. For instance, 1952 saw Ford convertibles outselling Chevy's by almost two to one: 22,534 to 11,975. By 1958, not only were the numbers substantially higher, but the roles had reversed: Chevy sold 65,157 convertibles to Ford's 51,876.

The Impala was one of the bright spots in a generally dismal 1958. Chevrolet built 60,000 of them (more than Ford

built Edsels) despite just two body styles, convertible and hardtop coupe. They were arguably the best expression of Chevy's determined move upmarket, with '58's larger, heavier body and big new 348-cid V-8. Fuel injection, which got more publicity than it deserved, had arrived as a '57 option, but high price meant few passenger Chevys were so equipped. Luxury was the key in the Impala class, and Impala succeeded. Like Pontiac did with its Bonneville, Chevy added pillared and pillarless Impala sedans to form a new top-line 1959 series. All four body styles, convertible included, were available with either a six or V-8. Chevy's '59 styling will ever be criticized, but its convertibles still outsold Ford's!

Meantime, the Chevy Corvette had gone from sales chump to sports-car champ, partly by adopting convertible features. They first appeared on the '56s, along with curvy new styling that completely did away with the former "bathtub" look. The '57s were outwardly unchanged but went faster, thanks to that year's enlarged 283-cid small-block and optional fuel injection that offered up to a like number of horses. Handling

improved too. A bulkier, weightier body with four headlamps and more chrome made the '58 aesthetically less pleasing, but performance wasn't affected and volume went up. The '59s were treated to a minor cleanup and tallied 9670 units, a long way from the 3467 Corvettes built for '56. Chevy's sports car was here to stay.

A look at the production charts shows how badly Plymouth trailed in convertibles, not only behind the Big Two but the other GM makes and Mercury as well. (Plymouth convertibles usually accounted for only about 15 percent of those sold by the "low-priced three" in the early part of the decade, and as low as five percent later on). Despite a vigorous sales recovery on the strength of its stylish '55s and their new V-8 engines, Chrysler's breadwinner usually ran seventh in convertible volume. One reason: a hard-to-shake conservative image. In this, Plymouth was even worse off than Chevrolet, which could boast more dealers and a "best-seller" tradition.

Plymouth rode a roller coaster in the Fifties. After Detroit's dullest '49 restyle, its 1950-52 models were little different

The '57 Dodge (above, a Coronet), received lines similar to other Chryslers, but got unique "swept wing" tailfins. The Coronet V8 was the line's lowest-priced convertible at $2842.

and their 1953-54 revisions weren't much better. The '55 was something else, though: shapely, colorful, and eye-catching, the work of Maury Baldwin and Virgil Exner. Plymouth was all-new again just two years later—the style leader of the "low-priced three"—and its V-8s were at least a match for the competition's. But soft-top sales didn't budge, perhaps because the ragtop got no emphasis. Even Plymouth's hottest, the 1956-58 Fury, came only as a hardtop coupe.

Through 1958, Plymouth offered only one convertible, in the top-line series as usual: Special Deluxe (1950), Cranbrook (1951-53), and Belvedere (1954-58). With such low volume, it made sense to standardize the V-8 for '55. The '57s were dramatic-looking and very impressive, the convertible wearing a special compound-curve windshield wrapped up at the top as well as around to the sides.

A second Plymouth convertible arrived for 1959 as a companion for that year's new Sport Fury hardtop, with up to 305 horsepower from a ram-induction 361-cid "Golden Commando" V-8. Big and flashy, the Sport Fury was what convertible buyers wanted and claimed over half of Plymouth's ragtop output that year, which itself was the highest since 1950. ▷

Right: 1957 saw the last—and possibly the prettiest—of the two-seat Thunderbirds. Below: Undoubtedly one of the gaudiest of all the '57 models was this Mercury Turnpike Cruiser, which (obviously) paced the Indy 500 that year.

Left: *No, we didn't mess up. This is the unique 1957 Ford Skyliner, a "retractable" convertible whose hard top folds into the trunk.*

*Restyled front and rear, the '57
Pontiac had more character than the
'56. It also had more power, as
Pontiac joined the horsepower race
in earnest; this Star Chief
convertible packs a 290-bhp V-8.*

Left: *Oldsmobile also restyled for
1957, and (you guessed it) upped
horsepower as well: Standard
across the board was a 371-cid
V-8 providing 277-bhp.*

The new star of the Pontiac line for 1957 was the fast and flashy Bonneville. At $5782 (almost $2700 more than a Star Chief), it came with fuel injection and 300+ horsepower.

Dodge was equally dull in the early Fifties but more interesting than Plymouth, thanks to several unique models. One was the low-price Wayfarer series of 1949—specifically the open three-seater with side curtains, which was thus technically a roadster. For 1950 it acquired roll-up windows to become a convertible, and looked more "important." Sales were never significant: 2903 of the '50s, 1002 of the '51s.

The standard Dodge convertible of these years was always in the premium Coronet series, which received the new "Red Ram" 241 V-8 for 1953. The name changed to Royal for '54, when 2000 were built. Included were 701 Royal 500s, a hot machine in the image of that year's Indianapolis pace car, supplied with chrome wire wheels, continental spare tire, special badges, and a 150-bhp Red Ram. Dealers could even specify a four-barrel Offenhauser manifold that made this somewhat dumpy drop-top a genuine scorcher.

While this 1958 Cadillac Eldorado Biarritz convertible (below) offered distinctive bodywork, at $7500, it cost $2000 more than a Series 62 convertible. Bottom left: 1958 DeSoto Firesweep; lowest priced convertible in the line at $3219. Bottom right: 1958 Dodge Custom Royal; $3298.

With a snazzy 1955 facelift, Dodge, like Plymouth, became a serious competitor again. From 1956 through 1959 there were always two convertibles, Coronet and Custom Royal— four if we count 1957's new D-500 option, which was available on any model in the line. This package gave you firm suspension, a 245-bhp hemi V-8 and 0-60-mph times of around nine seconds. The bold and rapid D-500 continued for 1958-59, though a wedgehead engine replaced the hemi. Offered with fuel injection for 1958, the 361-cid wedge produced 333 bhp, a new Dodge high.

Though DeSoto had some of its best sales years in the Fifties, its place in the Highland Park hierarchy was being steadily undermined by Dodge from below and Chrysler from above. DeSoto enjoyed record volume in 1955, almost outproduced Chrysler in '57—and was history by late 1960.

DeSoto persisted with one upper-echelon convertible through 1954, then expanded in a big way: a Fireflite and Firedome for '55, a special Fireflite Pacesetter for mid-'56 (100 replicas of that year's Indy pacer), a new Adventurer model for '57, and four different soft-tops—Firesweep, Firedome, Fireflite, and Adventurer—for 1958-59. Then...nothing, as DeSoto was left with a truncated line of sedans and hardtops for 1960-61.

The wildest DeSotos were the pre-1960 Adventurers, limited-production jobs with arresting color combinations, acres of anodized aluminum trim, and the hairiest engines (in '57, for instance, a 345-cid hemi with one bhp per cubic inch). Convertible production was very limited: 300 of the '57s, 82 for '58, and just 97 of the '59s—now collector's items all. They could fly, too: Fast-shifting TorqueFlite automatic took most Adventurers from 0 to 60 mph in around seven seconds

Above and left: *Famed for its failure, the '58 Edsel (here, a top-of-the-line Citation) was perhaps more a victim of bad timing than of poor styling. In Recession '58, it cost $3801.*

Left: Imperial Crown convertible offered a 392-cid V-8 with 345-bhp for 1958. Only 675 were sold at $5729, partly because this was almost $300 more than a Cadillac Series 62.

Below, right: *1958 Oldsmobile Super 88—in lavender. Chrome-laden, the '58s may have been called glitzy, but they were rarely called slow—not with up to 312-bhp available.*

Column at left, from top: *1958 Continental Mark III convertible being put through its paces. Note power tonneau cover and unusual back-cut rear window that matched the styling of its sedan counterpart. In 1958, it was yours for "only" $6283.*

and on to 125 mph or more. Torsion-bar front suspension gave these big bruisers surprisingly good handling.

Lesser DeSoto ragtops were hardly more numerous. In fact, the highest production for any V-8 DeSoto convertible came with the 1956 Fireflite: just 1385. Others are counted in the hundreds.

Chrysler Corporation is a leading convertible-maker today. But as the foregoing makes clear, its soft-top business was peripheral in the Fifties. This was true even for the high-priced Chrysler and Imperial, which had always done well with ragtops. Chrysler consistently offered two models—Windsor and New Yorker—through 1956, plus an Imperial version for '51, but annual volume never topped 3000 units from 1952 through the end of the decade. This is not to infer,

however, that Chrysler's convertibles were undesirable. In fact, the first drop-top 300, which replaced the Windsor for 1957, was a muscle car of impeccable breeding.

The '57 Chryslers were among Virgil Exner's best designs—gracefully finned and beautifully clean—though nobody knew then how quickly they could rust. Hemi V-8s and torsion-bar front suspension made them among the most roadable cars in America. The 300C convertible, with up to 390 bhp, high-grade interior, and unique frontal styling, listed at $5359 (close to $6000 delivered); just 484 were built. The following year's 300D notched up only 191 convertible sales, and 1959's wedgehead 300E scored but 140. The New Yorker, slightly less lavish but more affordable ($4600-$4900), fared little better: for 1957-59 respectively, 1049, 666, and 286.

*The burgeoning economy and general spirit of optimism that characterized the Fifties encouraged the production of prestigious, **affordable** convertibles. And despite their sometimes outlandish styling (or perhaps because of it), many of these '50s luxury yachts have become highly prized collector's items.*

Imperial became a separate make for 1955 but wasn't offered as a convertible until 1957. That happened to be Imperial's best year ever, the only one in which it would outsell Lincoln. Helping were 1167 Crown convertibles at $5568 apiece. From then on, the soft-top languished at 500-700 units a year as one ornate facelift succeeded another. The convertibles were as big and impressive as any Imperial but, despite heroic efforts, never cut heavily into Cadillac sales, the highest among domestic luxury convertibles. One problem was price: the Crown cost several hundred dollars more than a Cadillac 62, which had a more prestigious name and better resale value.

The Fifties were disastrous for all the independents. Packard's fate has already been mentioned. Partner Studebaker almost died with it, but was rescued at the eleventh hour (in 1958) by Curtiss-Wright, mainly as a tax-loss.

Car companies tend to cut back when the going gets tough, but Studebaker had cut out convertibles well before its mid-decade crisis. Its only Fifties soft-tops were thus the little Raymond Loewy Champions and somewhat larger Commanders of 1950-52. The Commander received a fine new V-8 for 1951, which gave its convertible real performance. What it needed was real styling. Studey was still plying its basic 1947 design, made bizarre with the "bullet-nose" facelift of 1950-51, more acceptable with the "clam-digger" front of 1952, the firm's centennial year. Relative to its size, Studebaker sold a fair number of convertibles. A shame it never found the money to produce an open version of the beautiful 1953

Above, left: *For 1958, Pontiac cut the price of the Bonneville convertible to $3586.* **Left:** *Now a four-passenger model, this 1959 Ford Thunderbird sold for $3979.*

Buick cleaned off much of the chrome from its 1959 models, instead gracing them with large, angled tailfins. This top-of-the-line Electra 225 convertible could be bought for $4192.

Starliner coupe, though that wouldn't have helped stave off the inevitable.

Nash built no large convertibles after 1948, but did produce a popular little one: the six-cylinder Rambler, which arrived in 1950 and was also offered as a two-door station wagon. Though its window frames were fixed and only the top dropped, the roofless Rambler won people over—perhaps because, at $1808, it was 1950's cheapest convertible. A total of 9330 were built for the model year. The convertible remained in production through 1954 and was always competitive; its price was up to only $1980 by then. As an economy car, it had no performance, of course, and its unit body was a devilish ruster. Still, America's first modern "compact" was pleasant as a convertible and, in its way, unique.

Arriving in 1954 to succeed Nash's small convertible was an even smaller one: the three-passenger Metropolitan, which also came as a coupe. Built in England with an Austin engine but resolutely Nash in appearance, the petite 85-inch-wheelbase Met enjoyed its greatest popularity in 1959, when over 22,000 were sold, about a third of them soft-tops.

A few Metropolitans were also badged as Hudsons. It's unclear when the last of these were sold, but the car simply became "Metropolitan" once Nash and Hudson expired in '57. Technically then, this was Hudson's last convertible. The big ones had ended in 1954. The last recorded production for Hudson soft-tops is 1952, when it listed 636.

All this is strange in a way, because Hudson seemed a strong proponent of convertibles. For 1950 it had no fewer than five: Pacemaker and Pacemaker Deluxe on a new 119-inch wheelbase; Super Six and Commodore Six/Eight on the familiar 124. The line was rearranged for 1951 and the potent Hornet arrived; it, too, was offered as a convertible, called "Brougham" (as were all drop-top Hudsons in this period). Even in 1953-54, the last years for "real" Hudsons, soft-top Wasps and Hornets remained available.

Hudson probably offered so many convertibles because they were so easy to build, sharing many body panels with sedans and coupes. Engines, wheelbases, badges, and trim were shuffled to produce the various permutations. All remained true to the original 1948 "Step-down" design, with strong unibody construction and that massive windshield header. And the Hornet, at least, was impressively quick—at 112-115 mph, America's fastest six-cylinder car. A pity more ragtops weren't built.

Willys-Overland brought out its first new car in a decade in 1952, but the handsome little Aero didn't come as a soft-top (evidently because it had unit construction too). No sooner had it appeared than Willys was swallowed by what was left of Kaiser-Frazer, which wasn't much.

The last of K-F's unique convertible sedans were offered as 1951 Frazer Manhattans. These were basically leftover 1950 Kaisers and Frazers "restyled" with new front and rear ends.

"Wide Track" Pontiacs sported modest fins for '59. The smaller of the two convertibles offered that year, this Catalina (right) is equipped with "Tri-Power" V-8.

Surveys of survivors suggest original production of between 128 and 131. Why so few? A high price—$3075—and a face only their mother could love. It was a salvage operation anyway, intended to rid K-F of remaining old-style bodies. Ironically, dealers could have sold 50,000 of the peculiar '51 Frazers, but only 10,000 were built in all.

As for Kaiser, its second-generation design for 1951 was all-new and beautiful, again the work of the artistic Dutch Darrin. Convertibles were mooted and one prototype was actually built, but the company would never have the funds to get one into production. Ditto hardtops, station wagons, and V-8s. These deficits, plus Henry Kaiser's intransigence and the money-sapping Henry J compact, culminated in 1955 with the departure of Kaiser-Willys from the U.S. car market.

All in all, even with the departure of the independents, this was a monumental era for the American convertible. The decade brought the proliferation of big, flashy, powerful cars that epitomized American success and self-confidence. Opulent ragtops had been seen before, of course (most notably in the Thirties), but their high prices placed them beyond the means of the masses. On the other hand, the burgeoning economy and general spirit of optimism that characterized the Fifties encouraged the production of prestigious, *affordable* convertibles. And despite their sometimes outlandish styling (or perhaps because of it), many of these '50s luxury yachts have become highly prized collector's items.

Plymouth's tailfins rose to new heights for 1959, as seen on this Sport Fury convertible coupe (right). Standard was a 260-bhp 318 V-8; a 305-bhp 361 was optional.

153

1960–69

THE PEAK
OF POPULARITY

1961 Oldsmobile Starfire

While there is little question that the '50s produced some of the most memorable cars of recent times – particularly in the later years – the decade that followed will be remembered as a "no holds barred" free-for-all in Motor City.

Buick softened its lines for 1960, but otherwise stood pat. The top-line Electra 225 (right) boasted 325-bhp and went for $4192, while the bottom-line LeSabre (below) had 250-bhp and sold for $3145.

For Detroit, the Sixties represent a high-water mark in automotive history. While there is little question that the Fifties produced some of the most memorable cars of recent times—particularly in the later years—the decade that followed will be remembered as a "no holds barred" free-for-all in Motor City.

No doubt many engineers and designers around at that time get teary-eyed reminiscing about the days before EPA, CAFE, crash test standards, and the like. "Anything goes" was the battle cry, and the war waged between GM, Ford, Chrysler—and yes, even AMC—was fought with reckless abandon.

The horsepower race seemed to have no finish line (though one was eventually drawn by the insurance companies), and new models saw real diversity for the first time in terms of size and powertrain layout. GM led the charge with such oddities as the Tempest and Corvair (failures due more to timing than design), and later started a revolution with the Toronado and Eldorado. Styling became somewhat more subdued, with enthusiasts seemingly divided as to whether or not it was for the better. By contrast, little argument can be heard against the continued growth and availability of sheer, raw power—the likes of which may never be seen again.

The result was more than just a bevy of what may be the best (and some say, the last) collectible cars to ever grace the hobby. Nineteen sixty-five saw a new yearly production record that would not be surpassed for nearly a decade; 1966 and 1969 were almost as good, and annual volume was never under seven million cars after 1962.

The Sixties were also the best years for American convertibles. Over half a millon were built in '65, a record that will probably never be equalled, let alone topped. Their heyday was 1962-66, when ragtops enjoyed a six-percent market share, up from only 4.5 percent in 1960.

Yet in the end, the Sixties were a giant game of Chutes and Ladders: By 1969, the convertible's market penetration had been cut by half. A few years later, soft-top models would account for less than one percent of all Detroit cars.

The Sixties convertible leaders were remarkably constant. With one exception, the top five producers were always the same: Chevrolet, Ford, Pontiac, Buick, and Oldsmobile, which finished in that order in five of the 10 model years. The exception was 1961, when Cadillac built a few more convertibles than Olds. In 1965-66, largely on the strength of its popular new Mustang, Ford managed to build more soft-tops than Chevy. Once the "ponycar" craze subsided, though, Chevrolet was again the convertible leader, and in 1968-69, Pontiac ran second, ahead of Ford.

Independents were hardly in the convertible business during the Sixties, mainly because there were hardly any independents left. Let's begin with their story.

Studebaker-Packard (renamed Studebaker Corporation in 1962) returned to convertibles for 1960 with a compact Lark offering, its first soft-top in eight years. At 8571 units, model year production was rather good, considering the South Bend automaker hadn't built that many convertibles a year since 1950. But the pace wouldn't last. Regarding Studebaker's and Rambler's initial success with compacts, one could paraphrase automotive writer Rich Taylor: Independents are sometimes capable of stealing a march on giant manufacturers, but before they know it, they have elephant footprints all over them.

Styled by Duncan McRae, the pert and practical Lark was a clever, shortened, and reskinned update of Studebaker's old 1953-58 sedan/wagon platform (several years of huge deficits precluded an all-new design). It arrived for 1959, when people were turning away from Detroit dinosaurs and toward imports like the seemingly preposterous Volkswagen. Big Three

compacts were then a year off, so Studebaker shared the domestic small-car market only with Rambler, which was doing even better. People who wouldn't have been caught dead in a Studebaker showroom a year earlier scrambled to buy Larks in '59. Studebaker calendar year production rose from 45,000 in 1958 to over 126,000, providing the automaker with an unaccustomed profit.

The Lark was a good product, available with Studebaker's old L-head six or its somewhat younger—and still spunky—259 V-8. From the first, Studebaker wisely offered several body styles: two-door wagon, hardtop coupe, and two- and four-door sedans. The new-for-'60 convertible came only in upmarket Regal trim at starting prices of $2600-$2700. The '61 version was little changed apart from slightly squarer contours. Unfortunately, neither the convertible nor the Lark line as a whole could maintain their strong initial sales. Between formidable rivalry from the Falcon/Corvair/Valiant trio and certain problems of its own, Studebaker could only watch its sales plunge. For 1964, the last year of domestically built

Studebakers, total production was only 37,000. Aside from an elderly basic design (and despite Brook Stevens' nice facelifts for 1962 and '64), the Lark was saddled by its inherited tendency to rust badly and fall apart. Because of this and Studebaker's increasingly publicized corporate troubles, resale values declined steadily each year. Then too, South Bend's dealer force was weak, and growing weaker.

For 1962, Studebaker added a bucket-seat V-8 convertible called Daytona, then put the label on all its '63 ragtops. But by then, the Big Three compacts all had convertibles too, and each undercut the Daytona's price. Studey convertible volume thus hovered around 2000 units for 1961-62, dropped to 1000 for '63, then to only 703 of the '64s, all V-8 Daytonas. Convertibles—and a good many other models—were dropped for 1965-66, when the firm departed South Bend and consolidated operations at its Canadian plant in Hamilton, Ontario. After that, Studebaker abandoned cars altogether. Though convertible versions of the sporty Hawk and glamorous Avanti coupes were contemplated, they never

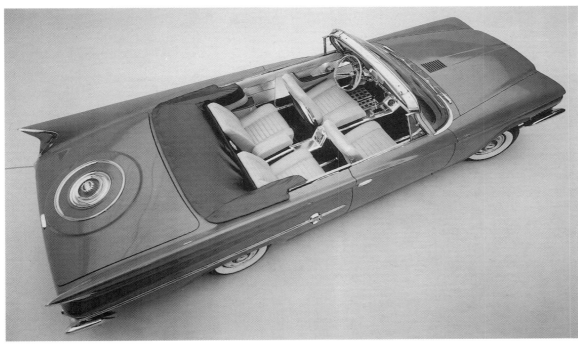

Above: *Edsel breathed its last in 1960, when it was little more than a stylized Ford. The Ranger was the only convertible offered: At $3000, a mere 76 were sold.*

Left: *Chrysler's glamourous letter-series cars carried on for 1960 with this 300F. Note fake spare tire indentation in trunk lid— it lasted only one year.*

By 1960, the Bonneville was offered in everything from station wagons to convertibles (right). Ragtop prices were down to $3476 and 17,172 were sold.

*Oldsmobile offered convertibles
in all three series for 1960, but
the Super 88 was the fastest: you
could get the bigger V-8 (up to
315-bhp) with the lighter body.*

went beyond the drawing board.

Rambler enjoyed much higher volume and a much better public image than Studebaker, George Romney's American Motors surprising just about everybody—including Romney—in the late Fifties. By 1960, Rambler was fourth in overall volume at well over 400,000 cars. In 1961 it displaced Plymouth as number three, then built a record 428,346 cars in 1963 (though that was good for only eighth in the industry that year).

Romney, who thought only of compacts, stepped aside as AMC president and chairman in 1962. New president Roy Abernethy looked at the company's volume and decided it meant that AMC should go toe-to-toe with the Big Three in every market sector. AMC tried, but only bloodied its nose—badly. This wasn't entirely Abernethy's fault, as AMC dealers were demanding a broader range of cars. At any rate, AMC's mid- to late-Sixties offerings—American, Ambassador, Marlin, Javelin, Classic, Rebel, and AMX—were ambitious but still not enough to compete fully with the much greater expansions of Chevrolet, Ford, Pontiac, and others. By 1969, its last year as a separate make, Rambler ranked 10th in industry volume at 250,000 units; other models grouped under the AMC marque accounted for about 175,000 more.

Rambler's sole convertible for 1961-63 was a 100-inch-wheelbase American model, attractively tagged at around $2400 base. The original 1958 American was a resurrected, slightly restyled 1953-55 Nash Rambler, a recession-market emergency measure. The '61 was simply a reskinned version, styled by craggy AMC chief designer Edmund Anderson so as to keep the old design going a few more years. A new

*The whole Chrysler line went
unibody in 1960, including this
Plymouth Fury convertible (right).
Fins were still in—but not for long.*

Right: *Cadillacs sported a cleaner (though still chrome-laden) front end for 1961. Two ragtops were offered: the $5455 Series 62 and $6477 Eldorado Biarritz.*

Buick made a radical styling change for '61 (right) by slicing off its once-proud fins altogether; convertible sales went down. Chevrolet did the same (below), but convertible sales went up.

convertible and hardtop coupe were part of the plan. But aesthetically, it didn't work, the cars looking very boxy and truncated. One English designer hired by AMC compared them to ordnance vehicles. Nevertheless, the American convertible turned a profit, recording 13,497 sales for '62 (the only year for which we could find sales figures). Far more efficient than expiring Studebaker, AMC was able to build this convertible to a price competitive with those of Valiant, Falcon, and Corvair models. That was the key to its success—along with the parent company's hearty reputation at the time.

Completely restyled by Dick Teague on a six-inch-longer wheelbase, the '64 added good styling to the American's list of attributes. Though bucket-seat hardtops had been available for a couple of years, the convertible continued in the mid-range bench-seat 440 series, priced at $2346.

With the convertible suddenly a serious salesmaker for the first time in anyone's memory, AMC decided to add Classic and Ambassador soft-tops for '65. Both lines were cleanly restyled that year, and the latter was stretched to 116 inches between wheel centers, 200 inches overall (a size that would have been an anathema to Romney). AMC called its '65s the "Sensible Spectaculars," but convertible sales weren't rousing: 12,334 for the three models combined.

Ambassador was officially a Rambler series through 1965, then registered as a separate AMC "make." Otherwise, the company's '66 convertibles were the same: one American, one Classic, one Ambassador. Classic became a Rebel for '67, and, along with Ambassador, acquired smooth new "coke-bottle" styling, one of Teague's best (and still underappreciated) efforts. Responding to the era's sporty-car craze, the American convertible became a bucket-seat Rogue ($2600 base) that year and the former Classic 770 was similarly transformed into a Rebel SST ($2800). The '67 drop-top Ambassador appeared in the lush, top-line DPL series ($3143).

Only the Rebel remained for 1968 (when that name achieved

165

make status too), though a base-series 550 convertible arrived ($2736), perhaps to make up for the loss of the American. Respective production was just 377 and 823 units. These would be AMC's last convertibles until the soft-top Renault Alliance of 17 years later. The Rambler marque itself ended after 1969, by which time AMC was switching to new names like Hornet and Gremlin, all registered as "makes."

Turning to the Big Three, Chrysler (the make) never seemed able to sustain its previous soft-top success in the Sixties. Indeed, the production record suggests that those who've glommed onto certain offerings had better keep them; there probably aren't that many left. Consider, for example, that production of the '60 through '65 300 letter-series convertibles never topped 625 per year, a peak reached in 1964; the '62 300H drop-top is particularly rare, as only 123 were made. Even some of the more "mundane" convertibles were built in very limited numbers. Any 1960 or '61 New Yorker, for instance, would have fewer than 575 sister ships.

The letter-series 300 never made any money. Perhaps it was never expected to, even after bean-counters replaced enthusiasts in Highland Park's executive suites. But the 300 did achieve its objective of establishing Chrysler as a builder of brute performance cars, albeit large ones.

In those days, Chrysler sniffed snobbishly at compact-toting competitors like Buick and Mercury, proudly announcing, "There will never be a small Chrysler." Minds would change later on, but it was a good sales ploy at the

Never a big seller, the Imperial Crown convertible (left) nevertheless hit a new sales low in 1961 at 429 units. Priced at $5774, it was $300 more than a Cadillac.

Right: *Monterey was Mercury's only convertible for 1961; 7053 were built at $3128. Below: A totally restyled Lincoln was offered for 1961, and its designers won awards for their efforts. The convertible sedan was the first one built in this country for almost a decade.*

time. In fact, contemporary market conditions didn't really warrant a small Chrysler, since Chrysler dealers also carried Plymouth, which had many smaller models—*too* many, in fact.

All the letter-series 300s were memorable, none more than the convertibles, available each year from 1957 through '65 except 1963. Big and bucket-seated, packed with power and style, they could show a clean pair of heels to most anything on the road, and do it right off the showroom floor. The original '55 C-300 had been built to make Chrysler stock-car champion, which it did until automakers agreed to stop emphasizing speed and cease competition sponsorship in 1957. After that, the letter-series became a sort of *ne plus ultra.* Though it never ran up many sales, it remained an important "floor-traffic builder" for Chrysler dealers.

Alas, the letter-series became rather tame toward the end, much closer to ordinary Chryslers in appearance, features, and performance. Then again, 1962's mighty 300H could be had with 405 horsepower, enough to blow off most any rival. And on its firm, race-bred suspension, it could embarrass many a foreign sports car as well.

Cast in the letter-series' image was a standard 300 series that replaced the mid-range Windsor for 1962. Engines were smaller and bucket seats cost extra, but prices were much lower and styling a dead ringer for that of the letter cars. These 300s were more successful, though not a lot. The most numerous of the convertibles were the '63s: about 3400 units, including 1861 specially trimmed "Pace Setter" models. The series hung around through 1971, always interesting and always with a convertible except in that final season.

Top: *1962 Buick Electra 225 came with the company's 401-cid V-8, and sold 7894 copies at $4366 each. Both figures were up slightly that year.*

Above: *Little changed at Cadillac for 1962; Fins were slightly lower while prices and production was slightly higher. A 325-bhp V-8 was still standard.*

Representing the upper and lower limits of GM's 1962 convertible line-up is the Cadillac Eldorado Biarritz at $6477 (left), and the Chevy II Nova 400 at $2475 (below). The former sold 1450 copies; the latter, 23,741.

Worth mentioning because of its novel looks and popularity among today's collectors is the "Sportsgrain" option for the 1968 300s: a swathe of wagon-like pseudo-wood trim along the bodysides intended to invoke the spirit, if not the "real-tree" honesty, of the Forties Town & Country. While nearly 1000 hardtops had this treatment, it was applied to only 175 convertibles. Both are now worth about twice as much as their unadorned counterparts.

Besides the non-letter 300s, Chrysler offered a low-line convertible throughout the Sixties: a Windsor for 1960, a Newport thereafter. When the non-letter arrived, the long-running New Yorker convertible was dropped. It had never sold well, New Yorker buyers evidently preferring closed models.

Of course, Chrysler-Plymouth dealers had the even bigger Imperial convertibles to sell in these years, but they didn't sell many: the peak was reached in 1964, with production of 922 units. These flashy land-yachts invariably appeared in the Crown series, a step up from the base Custom through 1963, the standard Imperial series thereafter. Styling for 1960-63 was by Virgil Exner, his fetish for Classic-era design themes apparent in big open wheel wells and, for 1961-63, freestanding headlamps encased in massive, chrome-plated shells. The 1964-66 cars were penned by Exner's successor, Elwood Engel, who brought in a Lincoln Continental touch from his work at Ford: squarish bodies with straight-through fenderlines trimmed in bright metal. Unlike other Chrysler products, Imperial retained a separate body and chassis until 1967, when production economics dictated a switch to unit construction. With that, Imperial increasingly became less distinctive and more a glorified Chrysler. Convertibles were the most expensive body style in the line short of the plush LeBaron hardtops and rarified Crown Imperial limos, selling well into the $6000-$7000 range—which at least partly accounts for

Opposite page, upper left: Chrysler planed off its fins for 1962, as seen on this $5461 300H. Opposite page, upper right: Dodge "downsized" for '62—about ten years too soon. This Polara 500 went for $3268. Right: 1962 Mercury S-55 sold for $3738.

their low volume.

Chrysler's junior divisions, Dodge and Plymouth, were minor leaguers in the Sixties convertible field, though the advent of compact Dart and Valiant models for '63 gave them much more soft-top business than they'd have had otherwise. The main reason is that sales of both makes' breadwinning full-size cars were greatly hampered through 1964. The 1960-61s were just too ugly to find much favor, while the 1962-64s were too small, the result of an Exner decision made long before the public was ready for "downsizing."

This involved reducing the standard Dodge and Plymouth to a 116-inch wheelbase for '62, making them 400 pounds lighter and six inches shorter than their predecessors. As automobiles, they were very good indeed, but the public rebelled at the smaller size and oddball styling, and sales plummeted. Plymouth finished eighth for the model year, a position it hadn't occupied since 1930. Dodge suffered less, partly by fielding a mid-year Chrysler-based 880 line (which effectively replaced recently deceased DeSoto on the corporate price ladder), then extended its "full-size" wheelbase for 1963. Thanks to more conventional styling, both makes soon recovered rapidly, emphasizing performance with 413-cubic-inch wedgehead V-8s for the street and special 426 hemis for racing (something competitors had also returned to by that point). With aluminum pistons and high-lift cam, the hemi developed up to 425 bhp, and in the light 330-series body won Dodge the 1962 National Hot Rod Association Championship. The hemi continued to rule the strips and, beginning in 1964, the stock-car ovals.

Big Dodge convertibles for 1960-61 comprised Polara and

By far the most expensive model in Ford's 1962 line, the Galaxie 500 XL Sunliner started at $3518. Standard was a 170-bhp, 292-cid V-8; the car pictured at left, however, has a 385-bhp 406.

Top: *The LeSabre line offered Buick's lowest-priced, full-size convertible for 1963. At $3339, it also was the most popular— save for the compact Skylark.*

Above: *Like Dodge, Plymouth fielded a line of smaller cars for 1962—with the same, poor results. The revived Sport Fury ragtop sold but 1516 copies.*

Left: *Thunderbird carried on for '62 with only minor styling alterations, though this new Sports Roadster was added at $5439. Only some 1400 were sold.* **Below:** *The Cadillac Eldorado Biarritz cost $6608 in 1963.*

Dart Phoenix models; 1962's were the mid-size Dart 440 and bucket-seat Polara 500, plus a big Custom 880. The Dart name replaced Lancer on Dodge's 1963 compact, which offered convertibles in mid-range 270 and bucket-seat GT trim. Priced under $3000, they were quite popular. Pushing hard at a sporty image, Dodge had no fewer than seven convertibles by 1965, its best year: the two Darts, Polara and Custom 880 models on a new 119-inch-wheelbase platform, and three in the mid-size Coronet line, a renamed, restyled '62 evolution. This broad allotment continued through the rest of the decade (and some confusing name changes).

One of Dodge's nicest Sixties ragtops was the intermediate Coronet R/T ("Road/Track") of 1967, an even livelier version of the previous year's good-looking, restyled Coronet 500. Standard equipment included bucket-seat interior, a 375-horsepower 440 V-8, heavy-duty "handling" suspension, wide tires, and oversize brakes. The hemi was technically available, having been reinstated as a production option for '66, but relatively few R/Ts were so equipped.

The Plymouth convertible story mirrors Dodge's. While Dodge production totals are largely not available, it seems that Plymouth built more open cars. Plymouth's first-generation Valiant (1960-62) wasn't offered as a convertible, but when the popular compact was redesigned for 1963 (along with Dodge's), it received two: standard V200 and bucket-seat Signet.

Plymouth's finest convertibles were reserved for the Fury line: full-size for 1960-61, mid-size for 1962-64, "standard" again from 1965. Beginning with 1962, a second ragtop was offered under the revived Sport Fury name, a swashbuckling bucket-seat performer with standard V-8. Two more convertibles arrived with the intermediate Belvedere/Satellite group of 1965, riding the 116-inch wheelbase deserted

Representing Chevrolet's ragtop line-up for 1963 are (top to bottom) Corvair Monza ($2481), Chevy II Nova 400 ($2472), and Impala V-8 ($3024). Also available: Monza Spyder, Impala (with a six), and Corvette.

Only a hardtop version of 1963's 300 letter-series (the J) was built, but the 300 Pace Setter commemorated the Chrysler pace car used for the Indy 500.

by Fury. Sharing their basic engineering with the Dodge Coronet, they were good-looking cars with squarish lines, clean sides, and lots of glass. The Satellite two-door convertible and hardtop were top of the Belvedere line and, like Coronet, could be ordered with a 426 V-8 developing 365 bhp and 470 lbs-ft of torque, though this was a wedge, not a hemi; that engine was available only on the race-intended Belvedere SuperStock hardtop (and Dodge's equivalent Ramcharger).

Apparently there was some moaning about this from Plymouth (and Dodge) customers, for the mighty hemi was made optionally available for selected 1966 intermediates, accompanied by oversize tires and brakes, and H.D. suspension. First offered with a four-speed, it was later available with TorqueFlite automatic. Although it was the lighter two-door sedans and hardtop coupes that took home the drag-strip trophies, the convertible Satellite hemi was the glamour car of the line—and fast. With the right tires and axle ratio (plus careful tuning), it could reach 120 mph in 12-13 seconds.

This package duly evolved into 1967's memorable Belvedere GTX, a convertible and hardtop coupe with standard 440 V-8 (hemi optional), silver-and-black grille and rear-deck applique, simulated hood air intakes, sport striping, dual exhausts, and buckets-and-console cabin. GTXs weren't cheap—$3500 base, around $4300 with typical options—but they were elegant muscle cars, among the best of that breed.

Of course, performance lovers aren't always wealthy, and Plymouth had a muscle car for them too: the whimsical Road Runner. Arriving for 1968 as pillared and pillarless coupes, it was basically a no-frills GTX—really stark inside and out. But Plymouth didn't skimp on the good stuff: a standard 383 V-8, firm suspension, heavy-duty manual transmission. The Runner did a lot for Plymouth in the burgeoning youth market, but inevitably became plusher and costlier, beginning with the '69s. Among the upgrades was a new $3313 RR convertible that sold 2128 copies for the model year compared to over 82,000 coupes and hardtops. (Dodge also fielded a "budget" muscle car that season, the Super Bee, but didn't bother with a ragtop).

After the disastrous downsizing of '62, Dodge resorted to larger models in '63. Two versions of the Polara ragtop were offered: base ($2963) and 500 ($3196).

Plymouth's one other convertible in this decade arrived with the second-generation Barracuda of 1967-69. The original Barracuda was essentially a fastback Valiant hardtop, announced in mid-1965 as a sort of Plymouth answer to the Ford Mustang (it wasn't, though the two cars arrived so close together as to make many think otherwise). The second-generation 'Cuda was longer-lower-wider and quite European in appearance. Though the 383 V-8 was newly available, the lighter, higher-revving 273 small-block was a better choice for street work. Both engines could be ordered with a Formula S package comprising H.D. suspension, tachometer, Goodyear Wide-Oval tires and special badges.

This Barracuda wasn't seriously changed through '69, but it seems to have been too late to capitalize on the ponycar craze that Mustang had uncovered overnight—and which began waning almost as quickly. Convertibles were the least salesworthy models, generating only 4228 orders for '67, 2840 for '68, and 1442 for '69. But that's the kind of volume that excites collectors, and the package itself was a

good one. The convertible 'Cuda continued into 1970's bigger and bulkier new third-generation, only to disappear two years later.

Although Ford Motor Company wasn't as dominant in convertibles as it had been in the Fifties, its Sixties soft-tops included some of the most interesting cars of all time. Notable was a revival of the convertible sedan, a body style not seen since the '51 Frazer. It debuted for 1961 as one of two all-new Lincoln Continentals.

Before it came the 1960 Continental Mark V, a continuation of the 1958-59 Mark III/IV, Lincoln-Mercury's attempt at a less costly, more saleable ultra-luxury car that would actually make money. As ever, the convertible was the most expensive model apart from the limousine, base-priced at around $7000. Still, it tallied only 2044 units.

But even as the first of these monsters was being introduced for 1958, the decision had been made to design an all-new Lincoln. When this appeared for 1961, the giant square-rigged Marks (and related standard Lincolns) were dropped. (The

178

Left: *Most expensive model in Oldsmobile's 1963 line-up was this Starfire ragtop at $4742.*
Below: *Compact 1963 Pontiac Tempest sold for $2564.*

General Motors was the company with the most to lose from the convertible's steady sales slide in the late Sixties. Four of its five divisions invariably figured among the top five convertible producers, and the fifth, Cadillac, was never far behind.

Top left: *1964 Chevrolet Impala SS; $3196.* Top right: *Buick Wildcat came standard with 325-bhp, 401-cid V-8 for $3455.* Above: *1964 Ford Falcon Futura Sprint was a mini-muscle car with its standard 260-cid V-8; $2671.*

Mark III tag would return, however, gracing a much smaller new 1968 personal-luxury hardtop.)

The '61 Lincoln Continental arrived in two four-door body styles: hardtop and convertible. Styling was the work of seven Ford designers who received the annual Industrial Design Institute Award for their efforts. Most agree they earned it. Though it looked unique, the Continental shared some tooling (especially around the cowl) with that year's equally

The 1964 Galaxie 500 XL convertible listed at $3498. Though a 289-cid, 200-bhp V-8 was standard, up to 425-bhp was available.

Restyled for '64 with squarer lines, the T-Birds sold better than ever, though convertibles made up a lower proportion of production; 9198 sold at $4953.

new Thunderbird hardtop and convertible, thus trimming production costs for two low-volume model lines. Yet the Lincolns were big (though much smaller and lighter than the 1958-60s) while the T-Birds were two-doors on a 10-inch-shorter wheelbase. Continental styling was crisp, chiseled, and elegant. Dead-on, the windows sloped inward toward the roof—the greatest "tumblehome" yet seen on an American car and one of the first uses of curved side glass in regular production.

Unlike K-F's convertible sedans, the Lincoln's side glass and window frames completely disappeared for a pure, uncluttered look. Likewise its convertible top, which stowed Ford Skyliner-style beneath a hinged rear deck via 11 relays connecting various mechanical and hydraulic linkages. Workmanship was first-rate. Customers also benefitted from the industry's most thorough pre-delivery testing and a then-unprecedented two-year/24,000-mile warranty.

Production models saw few changes through 1963. Wheel-base was stretched three inches (to 126) for '64, but the same basic styling was retained. The precisely assembled and balanced Continental V-8, a whopping 430 cubic inches, was replaced by an even smoother and more powerful 462 for '66.

As ever, though, the convertible was more indulgence than salesmaker, never amounting to more than about 10 percent of Continental production. It thus came to an end after '67 and the lowest convertible volume for this design generation: only 2276 units.

Lincoln's "other half" played a supporting role in the division's Sixties convertible business. Mercury soft-top production (all two-doors) peaked with the '63s: over 18,000, a record that still stands. But dealers never seemed to push convertibles very hard, nor were the cars particularly innovative. That's probably because Mercury didn't pioneer new products the way Ford and Lincoln did; if either make succeeded with one, Mercury might get its own version some time later. Mercury was thus unable to match sales with the

181

Often credited with starting the muscle car craze, the 1964 Pontiac GTO (right) came with a big 389-cid V-8 in an intermediate-sized chassis.

Despite sporty looks, available V-8s, and low prices (starting at $2670) this 1964 Daytona represents the last of Studebaker's ragtops.

Buick-Olds-Pontiac trio it had originally been created to compete with. Thing are different today, Mercury offering some distinctive cars all its own.

Mercury's early-Sixties big convertibles were peripheral low-volume models: a Monterey and Park Lane for 1960 (about 7500 units), a Monterey for 1961 (when series were shuffled and Park Lane axed, 7000 built), a Monterey Custom for '62 (around 5500). A "1962½" entry was the Monterey Custom S-55, priced $500 above the standard convertible ($3738) and much like it apart from buckets, console, and other sporty features then coming to the fore. Only 1315 were built, though. The completely restyled '63 ($3900) saw only 64 more.

The Park Lane and its convertible returned for '64 (Mercury's silver anniversary year), complementing a $3226 soft-top in that season's base-line Monterey series. Neither

Restyled for '64, the Imperial still didn't come close to matching its rivals in sales. One reason was price; at $6003, this Crown (left) cost more than a Cadillac. Below: 1965 Buick Wildcat Custom; $3727.

was numerous: 1967 and 2592 units, respectively. But volume improved for '65, when the big Mercs were restyled *à la* Lincoln and touted as "fine cars in the Continental tradition." The ragtop Monterey garnered 4762 orders, the Park Lane 6853. For '66, the S-55 returned as a separate series. Its convertible, priced at a reasonable $3614, saw only 669 copies. Demoted to a Monterey sub-series the following year, S-55 scored only 145 convertibles, then was canned.

Meantime, the soft-top 1967 Park Lane was down to 1191 units, the Monterey to 2673. After equally low numbers of '68s, the full-size Mercs were all-new for '69, when Marquis ousted Park Lane as the top-line series. A convertible continued there, a handsome beast and more Lincoln-like than ever, but volume didn't improve much, totaling 2319. The standard Monterey model was still around, though barely at just 1297 units. Mercury continued big convertibles through 1971, then gave up.

The Comet, Mercury's compact, received its first convertibles for 1963, as did that year's Ford Falcon. Bench-

seat Custom and bucket-seat S-22 models, offered at $2557/$2710, racked up over 13,000 sales between them, a big part of Mercury's 1963 ragtop record. After the 1962-63 Meteor failed to make the hoped-for impression in the mid-size field, Comet was elongated and embellished to fill in. A lone convertible was available for 1964-65, in the second-from-top Caliente series, priced around $2650 and good for just over 15,000 units a year.

For 1966, Comet became a true intermediate and offered three convertibles: the Caliente, plus base and GT models in that year's newly expanded high-performance Cyclone series. The latter were Mercury's rivals to the likes of the Pontiac GTO, Olds 4-4-2, and Dodge Coronet R/T. Powered by Ford's 335-bhp 390 V-8, the Cyclone offered a variety of useful suspension choices. The '67 was even more exciting with its new 427 option. Similar street racers were available among the all-new 1968 models—but not as convertibles, the Cyclones and Caliente being dropped in favor of a single offering in that year's new luxury Montego MX series; it lasted but a single

183

season. None of these mid-size Merc drop-tops sold more than about 2000 units a year except for the '66 Caliente (3922) and '68 Montego (3248). As we'll see, Ford did somewhat better with topless intermediates, helped immeasurably by the show-room drawing power of the Mustang.

Mercury was late in getting a version of the Mustang, but its new-for-'67 Cougar was smashing: longer and more luxurious than the Ford, identified by its "electric shaver" grille and sequential rear turn signals. Convertibles had to wait until 1969, when Cougar became longer and wider, somewhat fussier in appearance, and adopted ventless side glass. Like the original hardtop, the open Cougar came in plain-vanilla and XR7 guise, the latter with rich leather seat trim and comprehensive instrumentation surrounded by simulated walnut. Production came to about 6000 standards and 4000 XR7s. Perhaps reflecting Mercury's timidity toward convertibles, the hottest '69 Cougar, the new Eliminator, was offered only as a hardtop.

Ford Division may have abandoned the retractable, but it served up a variety of memorable Sixties soft-tops. Prime among them was the singular 1962-63 Thunderbird Sports Roadster—not a roadster at all but a special version of the normal open Bird.

While convertibles had never accounted for more than about an eighth of T-Bird sales, they were important image-builders. For 1961's third-generation design, Ford began considering how it might answer the constant clamor for a new two-seater. Lee Iacocca, installed as division general manager in 1960, approved the Sports Roadster as an inexpensive way to satisfy that small but vocal demand without tooling up a whole new body.

Designer Bud Kaufman came up with a fiberglass tonneau to cover the normal convertible's back-seat area, giving it faired-in headrests for the front buckets. He also overcame fitting problems so that the top could be raised or lowered with the cover in place. Kelsey-Hayes wire wheels were standard, and the stock rear fender skirts were left off to accommodate them.

The result was striking, but at a hefty $5439—$650 more

than the regular T-bird convertible—the Sports Roadster attracted few buyers: only 1427 for the '62 and just 455 for the near-identical '63. The model was duly cancelled for '64, though a similar tonneau became a dealer option for the regular convertible. (Few were sold.) Topless T-Bird demand peaked that year, then declined rapidly. Model year 1966 thus saw the last of the flock, 5049 in all. For 1967, the hardtop was enlarged and an even larger four-door sedan added, beginning the "big Bird" era that would last through 1976.

Mustang was a far more successful idea (one generally, though not accurately, ascribed to Iacocca). It took Detroit by storm with record first-year sales for a new model: 680,000 from its April 1964 introduction through the end of model year '65. Built to a price (about $2500 base) using off-the-shelf components, Mustang succeeded by dint of pretty, long-hood/short-deck styling and a myriad of options by which customers could make it anything from economy compact to road-burning grand tourer.

For once, a convertible generated serious volume: 101,945 units in Mustang's first, extra-long model year—15 percent of total production. The topless Mustang, in fact, was a big reason for the industry's record soft-top sales in '65. Yet this initial flood seemed to satiate demand. By 1967, the convertible was the slowest-selling of Mustang's three body styles, and was down to fewer than 15,000 units two years later.

A similar fate awaited Ford's other convertibles. The division entered the decade with a handful, had eight by 1966, then slimmed to six by 1970. In four years time there'd be none, though the convertible Mustang would be back.

Falcon was the biggest smash of the Big Three's original 1960 compacts: cleanly styled, cheap, reliable, and simple. Like Corvair and Valiant, it soon moved slightly upmarket with the help of folding-top models, but Falcon's wouldn't last long: introduced as a bucket-seat Futura for 1963, then dropped for '66 in deference to the Mustang convertible. There was also a Futura Sprint companion, a mid-1963 addition with standard buckets-and-console interior, tachometer, and Falcon's first V-8 option: the smooth, potent

The 1965 Dodge Dart GT came standard with a six-cylinder, but a 273-cid V-8 with 180-bhp was optional. Prices for the sporty ragtop started at $2628.

Largest of Dodge's 1965 convertible fleet was this Custom 880, which received new styling that year. Its $3335 price included a 383-cid V-8.

260-cid small-block, upgraded with more horsepower for '65 as the 289. Unusually modest production makes Sprint convertibles the most collectible Falcons by far: 4602 of the '63s, 4278 of the '64s, and just 300 of the '65s.

Ford's full-size Sunliner continued throughout the decade in the top-line series: Galaxie for 1960-61, Galaxie 500 thereafter. Bucket-seat 500XL versions were available from "1962½," renamed plain XL for 1969-70. The posh LTD, a new Galaxie sub-series for '65 and top of the line thereafter, wasn't offered as a ragtop until 1966, and then only for a year, when a lush "7-Litre" sub-model appeared with standard 428 big-block V-8. Just 2368 were built.

Most of these big Fords carried the workhorse 390 V-8. All were burly, luxurious cars on 119-inch wheelbases through 1968, 121 inches for the puffed-up '69s. Most were handsome, too, and none were really ugly. Peak production occurred with the '62 models—55,829 units—which reflects the dwindling interest in sporty big cars that occurred throughout the industry as the decade wore on.

The intermediate Fairlane, new for '62, was another Ford hit, if a somewhat smaller one than Falcon and Mustang. Convertibles weren't available until the enlarged second generation of 1966-67, when Fairlane 500, 500XL, and XL GT models appeared, the last with standard 390 V-8 or, less typically, the muscular 427. The mid-size Fords were completely redesigned for '68, becoming a bit larger and heavier and gaining curvier "coke-bottle" styling. Ragtops were down to two: a $2822 bench-seat Fairlane 500 and a $3001 bucket-seat GT in the new upper-crust Torino series. Fairlane convertible assemblies usually numbered 4000-6000 a year, though some individual models saw fewer. The '67 500XL, for instance, ran to just 1943 examples, the GT to 2117, the '69 Torino GT to 2552.

General Motors was the company with the most to lose from the convertible's steady sales slide in the late Sixties. Four of its five divisions invariably figured among the top five convertible producers, and the fifth, Cadillac, was never far behind. For 1965, the year Detroit built half a million ragtops,

This 1965 Mustang started the ponycar craze, and was one of the best-selling convertibles in history. Priced at $2614, first-year production totaled 101,945.

Sales of the Lincoln Continental convertible sedan (right) peaked in 1965 at 3356. Base price was the same as in '64 at $6938.

Top-of-the-line 1965 Oldsmobile 98 convertible (left) came with a new 425-cid, 360-bhp V-8. Priced at $4493, it sold 4903 examples.

The restyled '65s were the largest Plymouths in history, and sales of this Sport Fury convertible (right), priced at $3095, nearly doubled to 3858 units.

For the first time, Rambler fielded a
full line of convertibles in 1965.
Clockwise from top: American 440,
$2418; Classic 770, $2696;
Ambassador 990, $2955.

For the first time, Rambler fielded a
full line of convertibles in 1965.
Clockwise from top: American 440,
$2418; Classic 770, $2696;
Ambassador 990, $2955.

GM contributed more than 300,000, and well over a third of those were Chevrolets.

Mustang may have been the Sixties' most successful model, but Chevrolet was the decade's most successful make. For 30 years it had been the nation's best-seller; it remained so in the Sixties, no doubt aided by a steadily expanding product line that stretched in every direction—even up into the lower reaches of luxury-car territory. Naturally, this made for a great variety of convertibles.

The two-seat Corvette was always important in this respect, even after the classic Sting Ray coupe arrived for 1963 as an alternative to the customary "roadster." Helped by a $200-$300 price advantage, convertible 'Vettes handily outsold coupes through 1968. Then the coupe took hold, in part because it became a semi-open style—the first "T-top," in fact—offering much of the roadster's open-air feel without its usual drawbacks.

Corvette volume passed 10,000 for the first time with the 1960 models, little changed from the '59s. GM design chief Bill Mitchell gave the '61s a handsome new "ducktail," while the touched-up '62s introduced the 327-cid small-block that would be Corvette's mainstay V-8 through 1965.

Then came the Sting Ray, with exciting Mitchell styling on a four-inch-shorter wheelbase (98 inches) and Corvette's first independent rear suspension, engineered by Zora Arkus-Duntov. Sales broke 20,000 units that season, and continued upward each year except for a modest decline in '67. Styling

progressively improved too, and performance got a big boost from big-block V-8s beginning in '65, the last year for fuel injection and the first for optional disc brakes.

Corvette was rebodied for '68, becoming bigger, brasher, and more begadgeted. Motor-noters hooted it for that, as well as decidedly sloppy workmanship, but there were more buyers than ever: close to 40,000 for the '69s. By that point, the open Corvette started at $4438, up from 1960's $3872 base price.

Not quite as sporty, but at least of temporary importance in the soft-top picture, was Chevy's rear-engine Corvair—a failure in its original role as economy car, a sensation as a bucket-seat sports compact. Open Corvairs were first offered for '62 in Monza and new turbocharged Monza Spyder form. The pair garnered a healthy 44,000 sales the following year.

Unfortunately, the Corvair's promise and clever approach to efficient motoring was cut short in mid-stride. First, it failed to rival the new Mustang despite 1965's handsome, all-new second-generation design. Then it suffered a well-publicized attack from Ralph Nader, who condemned the '65 model for a fault in the 1960 suspension—something that had been completely fixed by '64. In any case, 1965-69 brought the last open Corvairs: Monza and, through 1966, a new uplevel Corsa model with optional turbo-power. The latter ran to 8353 and 3142 units for 1965-66, respectively. Monza began at around 26,500, plummeted by over half for '66 and sank to

Left: Chevy's full-size Impala could still be had with six or V-8 power in 1966. Prices for this popular V-8 convertible started at $3041.

Below left: Cadillacs were given square-cornered styling in '65, which was carried over for '66. That year's Eldorado ragtop would be the last—for a while.

1386 units two years later. Production of the final '69s: a mere 521.

Incidentally, Corvair convertible prices remained remarkably stable. The '62 Monza listed at $2483 base or $2846 in Spyder form; the '69 was less than $200 more. Today, the ragtops are among the rarest of Corvairs, and highly sought-after as both Corvairs and convertibles.

Other Chevy model lines were equally replete with convertibles. The full-size Impala series offered a standard bench-seat model throughout the decade, plus a sporty SS variant for 1962-67 (it reverted to option status for 1968-69). A similar arrangement prevailed in the 1962-63 Chevy II line, which arrived as the economy compact Corvair had failed to be. The Chevy II Nova and SS ragtops were dropped when the intermediate Chevelle debuted for 1964 with two

convertibles: Malibu and bucket-seat Malibu SS with a choice of six or V-8.

Then came Camaro, taking careful aim at Mustang beginning with model year '67. A convertible was part of its arsenal from the first. A few received the potent Z-28 engine/suspension package that won the Trans-Am Championship for Chevy in 1968-69. A sprightly performer with a wide range of V-8s and other options, the Camaro tallied upwards of a quarter-million annual sales in its early years and soon overtook Mustang. But GM design chief Mitchell never thought much of the first-generation design: "No damn good—too many people involved." Convertibles accounted for as small a portion of Camaro sales as they did Mustang's, and when Mitchell got around to creating a Camaro more to his liking (the second-generation design announced for "1970½"),

All GM intermediates got "Coke bottle" styling for 1966, including this Oldsmobile 442. Standard at its $3118 price was a 400-cid V-8 with 350-bhp.

Pontiac continued its GTO muscle car for 1966 preparing it for battle with a standard 333-bhp 389. The convertible sold for $3082.

Left: *The 1966 Ford Mustang was little changed from '65, but the newness was starting to wear off— "only" 72,119 were sold.* **Above:** *For 1966, the DeVille was Cadillac's only convertible. It sold 18,202 copies at $5608.*

it appeared as a coupe only.

GM's number-two convertible outfit—and after 1967, number two in the industry—was Pontiac, riding high on the sporty image established when Bunkie Knudsen became division general manager back in '57. Pontiac's commitment to the convertible market was enormous: full-size Catalina and Bonneville; compact and mid-size Tempest, Tempest Le Mans, and GTO; the Catalina-based 1966 2+2 and '67 Grand Prix (the latter a one-year-only version of Pontiac's big personal-luxury car with just 5876 built); and the Camaro-clone 1967-69 Firebird.

The legendary GTO was undoubtedly Pontiac's greatest Sixties convertible. Introduced in mid-1964—and, unlike many others of its ilk, offered as a convertible from day one—it

Plymouth restyled the Barracuda for 1967 (right) and sold 4228 ragtops; prices started at $2779. Car shown was fitted with '68 side marker lights.

started the muscle-car phenomenon that would soon sweep the industry and buyers off their feet. No wonder: With the proper options, a GTO could trim any other six-passenger car on the road.

To order a '64 GTO convertible, you began with a $2641 Tempest Custom or $2796 Tempest Le Mans drop-top, then plunked down an extra $300 for the GTO package, which included 389 V-8, quick steering, stiff shocks, dual exhausts, and premium tires. Four-speed manual gearbox cost $188, sintered metallic brake linings, H.D. radiator, and limited-slip differential added $75. Another $115 bought a 360-bhp 389; by that point, all you needed was a lead foot and lots of gas.

The GTO convertible continued past the end of the decade and always sold well for such a specialized car: up to 10,000 a year. In retrospect, it's the most desirable Pontiac convertible of the Sixties. Maybe ever.

Oldsmobile and Buick, while not at Pontiac's volume, continued to produce lots of topless cars throughout the Sixties. Oldsmobile consistently offered one in each of its model lines, from compact F-85/Cutlass to full-size 98. There was also a special Super/Delta 88 ragtop in 1961-66, the buckets-and-console Starfire. Its annual volume ranged from 2236 (1965) to 13,019 (1966), with 4000 to 7000 in most years.

Olds' answer to GTO was the 4-4-2, introduced as an option package at mid-'64, then made a separate model from 1966. A convertible was available each year. The designation originally denoted four-speed gearbox, four-barrel carb and dual exhausts; a 400 V-8 replaced the initial 330 for '65 and was factored into the "equation." The 4-4-2 package cost only

Right: GTOs got a minor styling update for 1967, and Pontiac replaced the 389-cid V-8 with a 335-bhp 400. Convertible prices now started at $3165.

about $250 that year, a bargain. Included were special road wheels; heavy-duty springs and shocks; beefed-up rear axle, driveshaft, and engine mounts; special frame and steering ratio; stabilizer bars front and rear; fat tires; 11-inch-diameter clutch; 70-amp battery and special trim. Performance was on the order of 7.5 seconds 0-60 mph, the quarter-mile in 17 seconds at 85 mph.

Each successive 4-4-2 was eagerly awaited. The 400 V-8 was never pushed much beyond 350 bhp, but it was enough. Especially in convertible guise, the 4-4-2 was good-looking and capable, a road car that handled and stopped as well as it accelerated and cruised. The '69s had big i.d. numerals, black-finish grille, and a set of hood bulges—a bit juvenile, but distinctive.

Occupying a somewhat more adult market sector with rather higher-priced cars, Buick built less extroverted convertibles than Olds and Pontiac, but lots of them. Like Oldsmobile, Buick had one in most every model line, from the compact and intermediate Special/Skylark through the big LeSabre, Invicta/Wildcat and long-wheelbase Electra 225.

The Gran Sport and Wildcat were Buick's most memorable Sixties soft-tops. The latter began in 1962 as a special Invicta hardtop. A convertible and hardtop sedan were added the next year; Wildcat then replaced Invicta for '64. Most Wildcats had bucket seats, and all were offered with brawny V-8s that ran to a 325-bhp 401. The GS, a sporty Special/ Skylark evolution, also began as a trim package, for '66, becoming a separate series for '68.

Buick's biggest engine yet arrived for 1967: a new 430 V-8, standard on Wildcat, Electra, and the svelte Riviera personal-luxury coupe. It had little more horsepower than the 401, but was quieter and smoother-running. Also new was a 400 for

Right: *Chrysler discontinued the letter-series 300s after 1965, so the standard 300 took over as the "sporting" entry. Standard at $4289 was a 350-bhp 440.*

Left: *Dodge's least expensive mid-sized convertible for 1968 was this Coronet 500. Priced at $3036, it came with a 230-bhp, 318 V-8; a 383 was optional.*

194

Right: *Ford's clean-lined Torino paced the Indy 500 in 1968, as this replica ragtop will attest. Offered only in "GT" guise, the Torino based at $3001.*

Above: *Mercury's 1968 Park Lane offered wood-planking decals for its flanks, lending new significance to the term "land yacht." Base price was $3822, about the same as Pontiac's big boat, the Bonneville* (right).

intermediates, appearing in a GS400 convertible and hardtop coupe; the open version started at near $3200.

Cadillac finished fifth or sixth in convertibles each year, underlining its traditional high appeal to moneyed luxury-minded buyers. This didn't require much model diversity either. Through 1966, Cadillac got by with one Series 62/DeVille convertible at around $6000 and an upmarket Eldorado Biarritz some $1000 higher. The latter vanished for '67, when Eldorado was reborn as a front-drive coupe, but the soft-top DeVille continued to account for about 17,000 sales each model year. This made Cadillac a major convertible producer, its volume exceeded only by that of ostensibly more popular makes like Plymouth, Dodge, and Mercury.

The outlandish tailfinned '59s soon gave way to more conservative Cadillacs, as the designs of new GM styling chief Bill Mitchell began replacing those of his predecessor Harley Earl (who'd retired in '58). The '61s were cleaner than any

Cadillacs in years. The make's long-running V-8 was revised for 1963 with a stiffer block, lighter and stronger crankshaft, and new accessory mounting points. All were notable steps toward the ultimate in smooth, quiet power, always a Cadillac objective. The major changes for 1965 were a lower silhouette and the end of tailfins. In 1966, Cadillac Division recorded its first 200,000 car year.

Studebaker excepted, the Sixties ended with the same automakers as had started the decade. For the convertible, however, it was a topsy-turvy 10 years. In 1969, just four years after scoring record production, convertibles barely made it over the 200,000 mark, and changes in model lineups and body production for 1970 suggested that their ranks would be thinner still in years to come.

In short, America's 1965 sweetheart had been spurned almost overnight. The reasons are not difficult to fathom. You'll find them in the next chapter.

Right: *The restyled Camaro for 1969 offered that model's last convertible—until the mid-Eighties. SS versions could now be ordered with a 325-bhp 396.*

Left: *Chevy's Impala convertible carried a base price of $3261 in 1969, but options like the brutish 427 V-8 could push that figure much higher.*

Right: *Mercury's Cougar wasn't offered as a ragtop until it was redesigned for '69. Base and XR7 versions were available starting at $3480 and $3692, respectively.*

197

THE FINAL SCENE

It seemed as though America was ending its love affair with the automobile. With ever-increasing social and government mandates, cars became less a statement and more a mere means of transportation.

*H*ow was it that the convertible, which had reached its peak in popularity only a decade before, would find itself hovering on the brink of extinction by the mid-Seventies? There are numerous theories, but in the end it all came down to one simple explanation: sales—or more precisely, lack of same.

It seemed as though America was ending its love affair with the automobile. With ever-increasing social and government mandates, cars became less a statement and more a mere means of transportation. To many, it started in 1971 with low-compression engines. Seventy-three and -four delivered a double-whammy in the form of ungainly impact-absorbing bumpers and an oil embargo that shifted focus from MPH to MPG. Many of the legends that once evoked passion even in people who wouldn't (or couldn't) buy them—Cobra Jet, SS, R/T—had passed on or were alive in name only. The final blow came in 1975, when Cadillac announced that the '76 Eldorado, by then the sole U.S. production ragtop, would represent the end of a era. The last example rolled off the assembly line on April 21, 1976—a date that came to be known as the day the convertible died.

Publications from business bibles to buff books waxed poetic over the drop-top's demise. All expressed their sorrow at its passing in grim eulogies that placed the blame on buyer apathy in hard times. But there were undoubtedly some less emotional reasons as well. Among the Big Three, car sales in general had fallen, and all were hurriedly developing "down-sized" models that could better satisfy the demands of the era. Buyers were turning to fuel-efficient foreign cars in the meantime, and the urgent situation left the American companies too busy to be worried about such frivolities as low-production convertibles. Furthermore, unibodies began to replace heavier body-on-frame designs, and many of these smaller, lighter cars did not structurally lend themselves to having their roofs chopped off. Added to that were forecasts of government rollover standards and suspected problems in mounting shoulder harnesses—neither of which materialized. In the end, however, it was bottom-line sales that caused the ax to fall.

1971 Oldsmobile 442

Nowhere was the buying trend more in evidence than at Chevrolet. The Corvette had been offered only as a convertible until 1963, after which the ragtop continued to outsell its coupe counterpart nearly two to one through 1968. Beginning in '69, however, the tables were turned. Despite the fact that the coupe was always priced higher, sales of the convertible dwindled to less than 15 percent of production by 1975—its final year.

As Mike Knepper, then editor of *Motor Trend* magazine, noted, "It's unfortunate some die-hard romantic in Detroit couldn't have seen fit to keep at least one convertible in production after this year." Indeed. But then, romantics are seldom captains of industry.

Of course, the big joke on all the doomsayers was that, as Mark Twain would have said, reports of the convertible's death were greatly exaggerated. Even before its resurgence at Chrysler Corporation in 1982, the ragtop never really died in the U.S.—not with topless imports from VWs to Rolls-Royces, convertible conversions of domestic coupes (which began appearing even before that last '76 Eldo), and the Jeep CJ. Of course, Iacocca revived the body style for money, not love, his autobiography notwithstanding.

Still, the fact remains that American "factory" convertibles were absent more than five years because they hadn't sold. But why hadn't they? Moreover, how could their sales plunge so drastically within five years of setting an all-time record?

Most affordable of Buick's full-sized ragtops for 1970 was this LeSabre Custom. Equipped with a 260-bhp, 350-cid V-8, prices started at $3700.

Pat Chappell, writing in *The Milestone Car* in 1976, said one reason was that buyers were offered a convertible alternative. The two-door hardtop, which first appeared in 1949, jumped ahead of the two-door sedan in sales volume within seven years, assuming a dominant role in Detroit production. She then quoted a leading consumer magazine: "While retaining the winter comfort of a closed car, the hardtop embodies the sporty look of the convertible...The 'ragtop' offers less protection than a hardtop in a roll-over accident. A convertible is expensive to buy, and added maintenance costs are likely to be high as well. The undeniable pleasure of top-down driving on ideal days may well be offset, in cold climates, by the undeniable difficulty of keeping the car

warm in winter." One wonders if they ever tried the heater in a Chrysler Windsor.

In 1972, that same magazine condemned the hardtop: "The 4-door sedan...is less given to rattles, squeaks, and drafts, it offers more protection in a roll-over accident and it's easier to get into and out of the rear seat." A year later, the magazine was pleased to report that "fewer pillarless hardtops are being sold," but was starting to worry about "a number of sedans with thin pillars." Apparently, the editors didn't think body construction had advanced much since 1949.

A second factor came into play around 1955: imports. Before the Volkswagen, whose sales first alarmed Detroit that year, foreign cars had been small potatoes in the vast U.S.

Above: *Rare (and fast) as they come, Dodge sold only 296 1970 Coronet RT convertibles. A 383 was standard, but this example has the famous Hemi—making it* **very** *rare (and* **very** *fast) indeed.*

Carrying into the '70s with a minor facelift, the Mustang ragtop (right) sold only half as well as in '69—7673 examples rolled off the line at $3025.

market. But many had been convertibles or roadsters—Jaguars, MGs, Triumphs—and experience with all kinds of imports began increasing buyer dissatisfaction with Detroit cars. The ranks of these customers swelled dramatically in the Sixties and reached monumental proportions by the mid-Seventies, which spelled big trouble for Detroit's market share in general and the convertible's in particular. In fact, the American convertible was exactly the type of car these people would have bought had they not been hooked on imports.

Take your typical 1970 "yuppie" (known back then as "fast-rising college grad") earning $12,000 a year, weaned on Oldsmobiles and driving a soft-top '66 Ninety-Eight.

Converted to imports by a friend's dead-reliable Bug or a neighbor's flashy Jaguar, he or she shops for a new convertible. But is it a $7000 Cadillac DeVille? No, it's a $2500 ragtop Beetle, a $3500 MGB or, disposable income permitting, a $7000 Mercedes 280SL. Bang! One Detroit customer lost, repeated many times.

We should also not forget the tragedy of Viet Nam, which claimed 57,000 young people and maimed thousands more. It's likely that many would have bought convertibles, especially the muscle-car variety. And we all know that muscle cars withered as much as convertibles in 1965-75.

A final nail in the convertible's coffin was the simple march

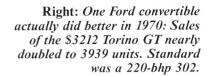

Right: *One Ford convertible actually did better in 1970: Sales of the $3212 Torino GT nearly doubled to 3939 units. Standard was a 220-bhp 302.*

of technology: the advent and almost universal adoption of more efficient and affordable air conditioning systems; sealing, sound-isolation, and other body improvements that really *did* render closed cars far quieter and more comfortable than convertibles; and the arrival of sunroofs and moonroofs, which provided seven-tenths of a convertible's feel with none of the inconvenience.

But enough sociology and on to the cars. Statistics tell much of the story:

YEAR	CONVERTIBLES	% OF MARKET
1965	509,419	5.48
1969	201,997	2.46
1970	91,863	1.40
1974	27,955	0.50

Considering its future role in reviving them, the Chrysler marque's early abandoning of convertibles is ironic. The 1970 Newport and 300, on the 124-inch wheelbase used for all

*Blessed with completely new styling
for 1970, sales of the Plymouth
Barracuda convertible soared—all the
way up to 2785 units. Sportiest of
the group was this 'Cuda at $3433.*

models that year except Town & Country wagons, would be the last Chrysler convertibles until 1982. A number of die-hards flocked to buy them, though too few. Only 1124 Newports and 1077 300s were built, all early in the model year. As an artifact, the 300 is to be preferred today. It came with the big 440-cubic-inch V-8, offering 350/375 gross horsepower. Newports had a 383, with the 440 optional. The 300's base price was $4580 against $3925 for the Newport, but a low-mileage original 300 is now worth 50 percent more than a comparable Newport—and both bring more than what they cost new, albeit in inflated dollars.

Dodge and Plymouth opened the decade with more elaborate convertible programs that dissolved in a hurry. Dodge's 1970 line included five ragtops in three model groups. The new 110-inch-wheelbase Challenger ponycar and mid-size 117-inch Coronet 500 contained base and sportier R/T models (the latter offering a 440 option). The 122-inch-wheelbase Polara V-8, that year's base full-size Dodge, carried a $3500 convertible.

The R/Ts were probably over-engined, especially the Challenger, though they did have carefully tuned (if hard-riding) chassis to handle the big-block's power. They remained the Detroit-style grand tourers R/Ts had been in the Sixties, but the market just wasn't there. Dodge yanked all but the base Challenger convertible for '71, and that was dropped the next year. Collectors should take note that Dodge's early-Seventies ragtop volume was modest, at best. For 1970: 4243 Challengers (of which 1070 were R/Ts); 1220 Coronets (924 500s, 296 R/Ts); and 842 Polara Deluxes. Despite being the only Dodge convertible left for '71, Challenger production was a meager 2165.

Plymouth's convertibles paralleled Dodge's except for an additional version of the hulkier, heavier new 1970 Barracuda. The Challenger, of course, was Dodge's belated ponycar, planned alongside the third-generation Barracuda but aimed more at Mercury Cougar than Ford Mustang. Both arrived for 1970 sharing basic underbody structure, chassis and drivetrains,

▷

Below: *Pontiac's big Bonneville received a less-than-flattering facelift for 1970, the convertible model's final year. (Later versions were part of the Grand Ville line.)*

Above: *Mercury Cougar grew larger in size (but smaller in sales) for 1971. Base and sporty XR7 ragtops were offered at $3681 and $3877, respectively. Combined sales totaled only 3440.*

A Dodge Challenger paced the Indy 500 in 1971, and 50 "replicas" were prepared for pre-race activities. Regular ragtops started at $3105; 2165 were sold.

though the Dodge rode a two-inch-longer wheelbase (110 inches) and differed in some styling elements. Both tailed off to just two closed models for 1973-74, then vanished.

Like Challenger, the third-generation Barracuda took a "more ponycar" approach to a market that was still strong at the time development work commenced. The new design feature for both was provision for big-block engines, up to and including the jumbo 440 and fiery 425-horsepower street hemi. So equipped, the ragtops bid fair as the fastest of Detroit's 1970-71 herd.

Partly because they were new, these Clydesdales enjoyed good 1970 sales. But ponycar demand was shrinking fast and GM's new Camaro/Firebird was strong competition, so both suffered mightily thereafter. Challenger sales dropped by 60 percent in one year, from 83,000 for 1970 to some 30,000 of the '71s. Barracuda fared worse, falling from about 58,000 to 18,690. In both cases, most of those sold were hardtop coupes.

The 1970 Barracudas comprised hardtop and convertible in standard, luxury Gran Coupe, and performance-oriented 'Cuda trim—meaning that, yes, you could buy a "Gran Coupe convertible," though only in 1970. Ragtop prices that year ran $3034 to $3433. The standard cars came with a six; Gran Coupes carried the venerable 318 V-8 as standard, the muscle-laden 'Cudas a 383. Like Dodge, Plymouth offered standard and sporty intermediate convertibles and one full-size model for 1970. Respectively, these were Satellite, Road Runner, and Fury III. The mid-size GTX and big Sport Fury models did not return from '69. The Satellite name had replaced Belvedere on Plymouth intermediates for '68, the year Road Runner was introduced. The '70 line marked the last of this mid-size generation—and mid-size Plymouth ragtops.

All of which makes the 1970 RR convertible a highly desirable collector's item today. Named for the beloved Warner Brothers cartoon character, the Runner still came with cartoon decals and "beep-beep" horn. As before, the '70 lived up to that name: Tightly sprung, it cornered as if on rails and went like almighty clappers when asked to (which was most of the time for many owners). V-8s were the same stalwart array 'Cudas offered, including the street hemi.

But 1972's swoopy new-generation design gave Chrysler a convenient excuse for forgetting mid-size Dodge and Plymouth convertibles, hence their termination. As a hardtop, the Road Runner would survive through 1975. Then Chrysler abandoned performance cars across the board and the Runner became a "paint-on performance" version of the compact Volare—about which the less said the better.

The Fury III was Plymouth's best-selling soft-top in these years, the top of the full-size line ($3415 for 1970) save the hardtop Sport Fury GT and exotic Superbird. But it was all relative: Plymouth convertible volume shrunk just like Dodge's.

For 1970, the tally was: Barracuda, 1554; Barracuda Gran Coupe, 596; 'Cuda, 636; Satellite, 701; Road Runner, 824; Fury III, 1952. Only the Barracuda returned for '71, selling a paltry 1388 units (374 of which were the sporty 'Cuda model).

For Ford Motor Company, it was, as the philosopher said, a case of "the same story, only more so." The convertible took longer to die at Dearborn, but the handwriting was on the wall. Lincoln had given up after 1967; Mercury averaged about 4000 a year in 1970-73, Ford about 13,000. By that point, the only ones left were Mustang and Cougar. Both were scrubbed for '74, when Cougar became a fat-cat intermediate and the original ponycar was replaced by the underwhelming Mustang II.

The end of the drop-top Mustang seemed inconceivable, for the convertible had been a big part of Mustang's early success. Though it found fewer buyers as the years passed, it was always there, touted with let-them-eat-cake praise and

Left: *Despite generally declining convertible sales, Chevy built more Impala ragtops in 1972 than in '71; 6456 to be exact. With a standard V-8, they cost $3979.*

Above: *1972 would prove to be the last year for the Oldsmobile 442 convertible, which was now just a Cutlass Supreme option package.*

Left: *Detroit rarely missed the opportunity to produce replicas of Indy 500 pace cars, and Oldsmobile was no exception. At left is a 1972 Hurst Olds.*

prominent in the brochures. Maybe it doesn't sell, Ford seemed to be saying, but it sure helps Mustang's image.

And Ford product planners gave the convertible their best possible shot. Unlike Chrysler and GM rivals, the topless Mustang was never diluted by sub-models. There was always just one, albeit with the usual long list of options, including wild engines. And it did have a following, a much larger one than other roofless ponycars. When Ford announced that the 1973 Mustang ragtop would be the last, dealers moved close to 12,000, 50 percent more than the annual total for 1970-72.

Ford's other convertibles were a prosaic lot, few in number, and sooner extinct. The intermediate Torino, restyled for 1970, offered its last soft-top for '71, a GT model (1613 sold). The full-size Ford did better, recording 6348 XL sales for 1970 and 5750/4234 for 1971-72, when it finally shifted to the top-line LTD series. Unabashedly big and luxurious, the LTD started at $4500 and was typically optioned to well over $5000.

Predictably, Mercury still mostly followed Ford's convertible strategy. An exception was continuation of standard and XR-7 Cougars for 1970-73. Priced about $500 above the soft-top Mustang, they still aimed at better-heeled types. Trouble was, few such buyers seemed to want convertibles now. Though much larger and heavier than the original, these Cougars were nice-looking, well-appointed cars but 4000 units a year was hardly impressive volume for an outfit like Lincoln-Mercury.

Unlike Ford, Mercury gave up on mid-size drop-tops after 1969. Its only other offerings were gigantic, 124-inch-wheelbase Monterey and Marquis models that respectively garnered 581 and 1233 sales for 1970, their final year.

The sheer size and product spread of General Motors virtually assured that the world's largest automaker would field the most convertibles of the Big Three and stay with them the longest. But even GM couldn't escape the market's turn from topless motoring. Its offerings thus dwindled from 18 different 1970 models to six by '73. Three years later, the Cadillac Eldorado would be the only drop-top Detroiter left.

The Chevrolet Corvette convertible persisted through 1975, though the companion T-top coupe had, as previously mentioned, surpassed it in sales in 1969 and took an increasing share of each subsequent year's pie. The final edition saw only 4629 copies, the lowest production for an open Corvette since 1956. Interestingly, Corvette performance took a dive at the same time. For 1970, a new 454-cid enlargement of Chevy's big-block V-8, designed to better meet emissions standards, replaced the previously optional 427s. But the most powerful (465-bhp) version planned was never offered because it couldn't be cleaned up enough to satisfy the "revenooers." For the same reason, the solid-lifter

Right: *1973 saw the last Mustang convertible–until the Eighties, that is. Starting at $3102, sales nearly doubled that year, when 11,853 were built.*

Special trim packages and "paint-on performance" were gaining favor in the early '70s, evidenced by this 1972 Mustang with the Sprint decor option.

350 LT-1 small-block option bit the dust after 1970.

Such changes took big bites out of Corvette's top power ratings: 460 bhp for 1970, 425 for '71, 270 for '72 (SAE net), 205 by 1975. This plus new federally mandated safety equipment made a change in the car's character inevitable. By 1975, Corvette had become a more balanced car—less outlandish, arguably more pleasant to drive—a plush high-speed GT instead of a stark straight-line screamer.

Yet sales continued strong regardless of the changes. Why? Despite its softer nature, the 'Vette was one of the few cars still available after mid-decade with anything like traditional Detroit performance. In short, "America's only true sports car" was now one of America's few really exciting cars.

Little topless material appeared in Chevy's other model lines. Through 1972 it consisted of a mid-size Chevelle Malibu and full-size Impala, base-priced at about $3200 and $4000, respectively, but selling for more like $4000/$5000 with popular options. The hot Malibu Super Sport was now an option package, but could be ordered with either the 454, pumping out 425 gross bhp for '71, or a 402-cid, 300-bhp V-8 evolved from the original 396 (and still called that).

GM switched all intermediates to new "Colonnade" styling for 1973, which meant pillared instead of pillarless hardtop coupes and sedans—and no more convertibles. Not counting the Corvette, this left Chevy with just the big convertible, built on the corporate B-body platform with a grand 121.5-inch wheelbase. Reasoning that it might as well shoot for the maximum buck, the division duly spruced up the Impala convertible into a Caprice Classic for 1973. It lasted only three model years.

Though it cost a lot—$4400-$4800 base, some $500-$800 up on the previous Impala—this Caprice was a nice car: roomy, luxurious, a smooth cruiser—and a dinosaur rapidly heading for the automotive tarpits. (In the wake of the 1973-74 fuel crisis, GM had decided to downsize its big cars, the first of which would appear, *sans* convertibles, for 1977.) But people liked it about as much as any convertible in those days, especially once they heard it was going away. The last-of-the-line '75 sold 8339 copies, the highest figure for any Seventies Chevrolet convertible.

As an artifact of how Americans once built cars, the Caprice Classic is about as good an example as you can find. Also worth noting: Clean originals now command well in

Left: *For 1972, the Cougar lost its 429-cid engine option, making a 266-bhp 351 the most potent available. Prices started at $3370; sales dropped to 3169.*

excess of their sticker prices, suggesting that all of GM's last big convertibles, not just the '76 Eldo, are inexorably becoming collectible automobiles.

Through 1974, Chevrolet continued to lead the industry in convertible volume, stunted though that had become. But with the end of intermediate and ponycar soft-tops, "USA-1" was overhauled in 1975 by Oldsmobile, which had been running it a close second. In fact, Olds built nearly half of all Detroit's 1975 ragtops and almost twice as many as Chevrolet. You could say that Lansing was among the final holdouts during the convertible's "last days in the bunker."

There was a reason for this, though only one: Olds had made a conscious effort to mop up most of whatever convertible market remained by mid-decade. By that point it had just one mop: a topless Delta 88 Royale, $5200 of full-size, 124-inch-wheelbase luxury cruiser that did what Lansing expected of it.

Contrary to some books, the convertible wasn't the most expensive Delta (some station wagons cost more), but it was certainly impressive. Tipping the scales at a portly 4300 pounds, it offered a healthy helping of standard features: power steering and front disc brakes, deluxe steering wheel,

Right: The top-line Pontiac convertible in 1973 was the Grand Ville, which listed at $4766. Below: Once exclusively a convertible, the ragtop Corvette accounted for only one out of every six sold in 1974.

At 3716 units, the Oldsmobile Delta 88 Royal convertible outsold its Buick and Pontiac rivals in 1974 — but just barely. Prices started at $4799.

steel-belted radial tires, and a 170-bhp (SAE net) 350 V-8. Styling after '72 suffered mainly from the 5-mph bumpers found on most big Detroit cars at the time — which gave it the prow of an 18-wheeler.

The Delta Royale was Olds' only convertible after 1972, but sales had been miserable until '75. All the publicity surrounding it (more, in fact, than attended the Caprice) allowed the last topless Olds to go out a modest success.

Royale aside, few other Olds ragtops survived past 1970. That year saw the last big Ninety-Eight. The next saw the end of the once-popular 4-4-2 muscle car, which reverted to option status for 1972. Like all others, 4-4-2 convertible numbers were low: 2933 of the '70s, 1304 of the '71s. The soft-top mid-size Cutlass, offered from 1970 only as a bucks-up Supreme model, said *adieu* after '72, though it managed a respectable 11,000-plus sales that year. Overall, Oldsmobile gave a dying breed one of its best shots, building well over 80,000 convertibles in 1970-75, second only to Chevrolet.

Buick and Pontiac turned in almost identical performances in the Seventies. Each division built about 15,000 convertibles for 1970, the last significant production year, about 8000 for 1971 and '72 and about half that number for 1973-75.

Five convertibles returned in the 1970 Buick line: the

traditional LeSabre/Wildcat/Electra trio, still on enormous 124- and 127-inch wheelbases, and the intermediate Skylark Custom and Gran Sport, the latter mounting a standard 455-cid V-8 with 350/360 bhp. Wildcat (1244 built) and GS 455 (1416) were the rarest, which naturally makes them the most collectible today.

The 455 was a kind of valedictory to the age of big-inch engines. Buick's largest ever, it had a compression ratio of at least 10:1 and returned only 10-12 miles per gallon of premium gas. The most powerful version was also used in 1970's senior Electra 225 series, which included the last Electra convertible. Minus that one, Buick's ragtops repeated for '71, except that the Wildcat series was renamed Centurion. Convertible sales were broadly lower, the Gran Sport sinking to 902 units, for example. With 1973's "Colonnade" intermediates and cancellation of the ragtop LeSabre, the Centurion was Buick's sole convertible. Then that series was dropped and the convertible became a LeSabre again, offered only in upmarket Custom trim. It, too, would depart after 1975, when production totaled 5300.

Like their divisional counterparts, the big '71 Buicks were as large as American cars would ever get. More rounded styling marked that year's new B/C-body design, with "fuselage" sides, massive hoods, and broad expanses of glass. GM's full-sizers continued in this form through 1976, with mainly minor annual changes to meet safety and emissions requirements. Then all were downsized, the first phase of

a corporate-wide "big shrink" that would cost a lot more than dollars.

Part of that cost involved a growing uniformity among GM's cars, reflected in its "last" convertibles of the Seventies. Strict market separation, the guiding principle of Al Sloan, had been sacrificed during the expansive Sixties in favor of platforms (in the necessary sizes) shared by as many divisions as possible. To some extent, this was prompted by demands from each dealer group for as many different kinds of cars as possible. But when the market contracted in the early Seventies, GM found itself with too many lookalike, overlapping model lines spread among five makes whose identities were no longer so clear to customers. The similarities began to hurt.

Nowhere was this more apparent than at Pontiac, which mainly marketed the same cars as Buick, Olds, and Chevrolet. (Only the names were changed to protect division executives.) Its convertibles thus followed the same pattern. For the record, Pontiac sold full-size soft-tops as a Catalina (1970-72), Bonneville (1970), and Grand Ville (1971-75). Typical yearly production was 3000-4500 units apiece except 1971-72, when the Catalina and Grand Ville saw fewer than 2500 each.

Also like sister divisions, Pontiac lost its mid-size convertibles with the 1973 "Colonnade" generation. It was just as well, as Pontiac could sell no more than 6000 of any one model in 1970-72. This made for some rather rare ragtops. For instance, the flashy high-performance GTO Judge saw

Probably on the strength of its "last year" significance, Buick's 1975 LeSabre convertible sold almost 50 percent better than the '74—5300 units all told—at $5133.

Cadillac Eldorado ragtop sales were up
slightly for 1975 (to 8950), despite
a 10-percent price hike to $10,354.
But neither volume nor price was near
what they would be in another year.

exactly 17 copies for '71, that year's normal GTO, 661.

Under division chief John Z. DeLorean, who claimed never to have made a mistake, Pontiac policy had been to outflank Chevy in the low-price field while challenging Olds/Buick in the medium-price ranks. But the results were an untimely blurring of Pontiac's "with it" image, a slide in assembly quality, a pile-up of unsold cars, and sales losses to Oldsmobile and Buick. In fact, Olds nosed out Pontiac in 1973 model year registrations, the first time that had happened since 1958; by 1975, both Olds and Buick were threatening Pontiac's number three spot. And while Pontiac had usually run fifth in convertible volume, Cadillac surpassed it in 1973.

Cadillac wasn't much affected by such intramural battles. Above the fray in its traditional luxury sector, it continued with a quarter-million or more annual sales in the early Seventies—and to make money with just one convertible. The 1970 model was still a 130-inch-wheelbase DeVille, priced at $6068 that year. Then, with 1971's new C-body, the DeVille was replaced by a soft-top version of the front-drive Eldorado, itself redesigned and grossly enlarged that year. At $7751, the revived Eldo convertible (the first since '66) was more profitable on fewer sales. A good thing, as yearly production hovered around 7500, versus 30,000-40,000 coupes. Nevertheless, as convertibles from other makes vanished, the Eldo came to be a prestige item for Cadillac; one even paced the 1973 Indianapolis 500.

But the deck was stacked against it almost from the first. For 1972, the Eldo hardtop appeared with a new "Custom Cabriolet" option, which meant an electric-sliding steel sunroof over the front seats and an elk-grain-vinyl rear half-roof (complete with "halo" trim molding). The more convenient sunroof, of course, was one of the key developments that hastened the drop-top's demise.

A feature dating back to the original 1953 Eldorado appeared on the '72 convertible: a metal boot or tonneau over the top well. Electronic fuel injection was optional by 1975, when Cadillac proffered another anti-convertible idea: the Astro Roof, a tinted-glass power moonroof with sliding interior sunshade.

The funeral notices for the American convertible mentioned at the beginning of this chapter were prompted by Cadillac's announcement that the '76 Eldorado convertible would be the last. The division even announced production in advance: 14,000—up nearly 60 percent on the '75 total. While that represented the number of convertible tops and mechanisms left in stock, Cadillac was clearly milking this

"milestone" for all its worth.

Gripped by last-chance acquisitiveness, buyers beat down the doors—and, figuratively, each other sometimes. "We expect to sell every one," said then general manager Edward C. Kennard. "I've already received letters from people saying they want to buy the last one. Maybe we should make the last 2000 the same, call it the 'Finale' and get another $200 or $300 for it." (And they wonder why we have consumer advocates.)

Ultimately, the decision was to single out the last *200*. All were painted white and had white tops, wheel covers, and upholstery, plus a special dash plaque attesting to "the end of an era."

The '76 Eldorado convertibles, the last 200 in particular, thus became the subjects of a sales stampede the likes of which are seldom seen in the automotive world. Would-be owners began offering well over sticker, which was about $12,000, thus sending delivered prices toward the moon. Dealers, meantime, had naturally stocked up against the expected onslaught of these suckers. Ignorant "money" magazines, the more ignorant general media, and even the National Automobile Dealers Association *Used Car Guide* touted '76 values well above those for the '75s—as much as *eight years* after they were built.

Unheard in this near hysteria were the voices of experienced car collectors and organizations like the Cadillac-LaSalle Club and Milestone Car Society. The '76 Eldorado convertible, they warned, was about 50 percent more common than the '75; ready-made collector's items are rarely good investments; and new convertibles were still being built if you counted AMC's Jeeps or the imports.

But buyers didn't listen, of course, some paying up to $30,000 for one of these "last convertibles"—proving once again that P.T. Barnum was right about the birth rate of the easily duped. Today, a '76 Eldo convertible is worth little more than a '75 in comparable condition.

In 1984, a rather ridiculous lawsuit cropped up when a couple of lawyers filed a class-action suit against Cadillac on behalf of all who'd bought '76s as investments. Reason? The division had "promised" that the '76 Eldorado would be its last convertible, and here Cadillac was offering them again. Little has been heard of the suit since, which is about what it deserves.

Of course, Cadillac wasn't alone with a revived convertible in 1984. But that story, and the tale of the ragtop's rebirth throughout Detroit, deserves a separate chapter—which is what we give it.

Above: *Though the car pictured is actually a 1975 Eldorado, the last 200 '76s were finished in the same color scheme: white on white on white.*

Left: *Now* this *is a 1976 Eldorado. How can one tell? The Cadillac logo and trim strip above the grille are different. 14,000 were built.*

RISING FROM
THE ASHES

Although Lee Iacocca and Chrysler Corporation are generally credited with the ragtop's revival, they were not the sole revelers. Buick introduced a limited-production Riviera convertible at about the same time, though its impact wasn't nearly as great. Buick's offering notwithstanding, history will undoubtedly give Chrysler and Iacocca the kudos—besides, theirs makes for a better story.

*I*n contrast to the bleak times associated with the late Seventies, the '80s dawned with much automotive promise. Chrysler Corporation, which had been riding a sales slide to the brink of disaster, was being revived by Lee Iacocca— with the help of a few billion dollars of the taxpayers' money. Effects of the second gas crisis (like wars, we had now begun to number them), which once again altered driving and buying habits in 1979, began to fade from memory. Technology was finally catching up with the demands of government regulations, effectively erasing "performance" from the automotive dictionary of dirty words.

In short, the future again looked bright. And with this optimism came enthusiasm, which in turn brought the resurrection of the muscle car—and the convertible.

Although Lee Iacocca and Chrysler Corporation are generally credited with the ragtop's revival, they were not the sole revelers. Buick introduced a limited-production Riviera convertible at about the same time, though its impact wasn't nearly as great. Buick's offering notwithstanding, history will undoubtedly give Chrysler and Iacocca the kudos—besides, theirs makes for a better story.

The legend of how Iacocca (after being ungratefully canned by Henry Ford II) rode off to save the ailing Chrysler Corporation has almost become part of American folklore— mainly because Iacocca put it there in his own best-selling autobiography. Of course, history will treat Iacocca kindly because, to paraphrase Sir Winston Churchill, he wrote so much of it himself.

In said autobiography, Iacocca gives this account of the events leading up to the ragtop's revival: "In 1982, as we began

1989 Chrysler TC by Maserati

221

*The Dodge 400 (below), along with
its Chrysler LeBaron stablemate,
was first introduced in the spring
of 1981—just in time for the
summer selling season.*

*Very little changed for '83,
(below) except that the price
increased $200 to $12,500.
Production during the model year
reached 4888 units.*

*Chrysler gained some stiff
competition in 1983. The revived
Mustang convertible (above) sold
23,438 copies its first year, at
a base price of $12,467.*

to get healthy again, I decided to bring back the convertible," he wrote. "As an experiment, I had one built by hand from a Chrysler LeBaron. I drove it over the summer, and I felt like the Pied Piper. People in Mercedes and Cadillacs started running me off the road and pulling me over like a cop. 'What are you driving?' they all wanted to know. 'Who built it? Where can I get one?'

"When they recognized my now familiar face behind the wheel [courtesy of TV commercials] they would sign up for one right on the spot. I drove to my local shopping center one day, and a big crowd gathered around me and my convertible. You would have thought I was giving away $10 bills! It didn't take a genius to see that this car was creating a great deal of excitement.

Above: *Buick introduced a Riviera convertible at almost the same time as Chrysler, but at $25,000, few were sold and it was dropped after 1985.*

Left: *Pontiac also joined the ragtop revival in late 1983 with its 2000, later known as the Sunbird. 626 were sold during its abbreviated first year.*

"Back at the office, we decided to skip the research. Our attitude was: 'Let's just build it. We won't make any money, but it'll be great publicity. If we're lucky, we'll break even...' Turned out, we sold 23,000 the first year instead of the three thousand we had planned.

"Before long, GM and Ford were bringing out convertibles of their own. In other words, little old Chrysler was now leading the way instead of bringing up the rear."

To this, a few additions and corrections. As mentioned earlier, Chrysler wasn't alone in the convertible's 1982 revival. That same year, Buick introduced a new soft-top Riviera, the first ever, converted from Riv coupes by Cars & Concepts, the Brighton, Michigan, design and fabrication house that assisted Chrysler with its convertibles.

Furthermore, the decision to offer convertibles had almost certainly been made by the time that crowd gathered around Chairman Lee's one-off. It was not a case of, as some joked about the K, "if this one sells, we'll build another one." Also, he must have meant the summer of '81, as his production convertibles were in dealer showrooms by the summer of '82, having been introduced that spring.

But what's important is that the convertible was back. Strategically introduced in time for the annual spring sales push (one of Iacocca's favored sales tactics at Ford in the Sixties), Chrysler fielded a pair based on the new-for-'82 Chrysler LeBaron/Dodge 400. The first of many K-car variations to come, these were plusher, pricier, and slightly longer than Aries/Reliant but otherwise identical, riding the

223

same 100.3-inch-wheelbase chassis. The ragtops came with the 2.6-liter Mitsubishi four optional on lesser models, and with its associated three-speed automatic transaxle.

Business proved good, if not booming. (Iacocca's claimed 23,000 sales reflects combined LeBaron/400 volume for 1982 *and* '83). But it was strong enough that Chrysler's St. Louis plant, which supplied the coupes for convertible conversion, began converting some itself when C&C couldn't keep up. Eventually, St. Louis took over the job entirely.

The auto editors of CONSUMER GUIDE® first tried one of these reborn convertibles, a Dodge 400, in late 1982. "It's still a real kick to put the top down and go cruising on a sunny day," they wrote. "The standard power top worked flawlessly... Expensive-looking vinyl trim and carpets gave the interior a quality appearance and are standard [but the] dashboard comes only with speedometer and fuel gauge and long pieces of fake wood... The test model had only 2000 miles on it [yet] the top was already wrinkled [and the] zip-out plastic back window was starting to scratch and will probably need replacement before the last payment is made."

Things weren't much better on the road: "With the top up, wind whistles through the interior at highway speed. Wind

and road noises combine with body shakes for a lot of racket. There are large blind spots to the rear...doors feel heavy from reinforcing and are hard to close tightly. Chrysler claims the [conversion] adds little weight, but the car feels sluggish and underpowered...The convertible conversion eats up so much rear seat room that it's nearly impossible for adults to sit in back."

The editors admitted that most of these faults were typical of convertibles since time immemorial, and that the true ragtop nut would probably be willing to put up with them. But their conclusions were still mixed: "Viewed as a car for show, it's a great success. The striking appearance nearly disguises its K-car origins. As a car for go, it leaves a great deal to be desired."

Chrysler set about making its ragtops more desirable. First came a new Town & Country model for '83, the first open T&C since 1949 and a car that seemed sure to please those with a sense of history. True, its flanks were adorned with plastic instead of real tree-wood, but even the original had used mahogany decals from mid-1947. Maintaining tradition, the new T&C was expensive—$16,300 initially—though that was almost exactly equivalent (in much-inflated dollars) to the

Top: *Cadillac brought back the Eldorado convertible in 1984, much to the displeasure of those who squirreled away their '76s as investments. The '84 cost a whopping $32,000.* **Right:** *1984 Chrysler LeBaron; $11,595.*

Chrysler revived the Town & Country name from the '40s when it introduced a ritzy, leather-lined, wood-sided convertible in 1984 that sold for $16,300.

'49 model's $3995. Newly optional for both ragtop LeBarons was a handsome Mark Cross package comprising leather interior trim (unfortunately festooned with "MC" logos), cast-aluminum road wheels, more instruments (electronic, alas), and more, yours for $2800.

The '84 Chrysler convertibles answered some of *CG*'s objections. A more compact top mechanism liberated additional back-seat space, new roll-down rear quarter windows reduced the big over-the-shoulder blind spot, and the backlight switched from plastic to glass. Dodge 400s became 600s for '84 and '85 and brought a new 600ES Turbo convertible with the blown, 147-horsepower version of Chrysler's own 2.2-liter four. A special sport/handling suspension package was standard, bringing larger front and rear anti-roll bars, "high-control" shocks, firmed-up power steering, and 60-series performance tires on "Swiss cheese" aluminum wheels. Base price was near $14,000.

For 1986, LeBaron and 600 were slightly restyled at each end and offered a second engine option: the new 2.5-liter version of Chrysler's "Trans-4," smoother than the base 2.2 by way of a Mitsubishi-style balancer shaft. But then both these "CV-Series" convertibles were cancelled for '87, leaving Dodge

dealers with no ragtops and Chrysler-Plymouth stores with a handsome new LeBaron. (As consolation to the Dodge boys, Chrysler cancelled its Laser version of Dodge's Daytona sports coupe, which was heavily facelifted for good measure.)

There was a reason, of course: greater distinction between Dodge and C-P through fewer shared models. And the new J-body LeBaron was Chrysler's best-looking convertible yet: smooth, rounded, and aerodynamic, a testimony to the talent of Chrysler's stylists under Tom Gale. The T&C treatment didn't suit the new look and was abandoned, but the "Premium" convertible (the only model offered in '87) included a host of standard equipment, including the 2.5 engine (2.2 turbo was optional), all for under $14,000.

Still, this was basically a K-car underneath, and CONSUMER GUIDE® noted that it wasn't "overwhelmed by the LeBaron's road manners, interior materials, or assembly quality"—nor the turbo 2.2, which "generates 46 more horsepower [than the 2.5] and a good deal more noise as well." Nevertheless, it was an improved car overall.

For 1988, the Premium model was dressed up even further, gaining automatic temperature control, automatic transmission, power (and heated) outside mirrors, and

Some improvements were made to Chrysler's 1984 convertibles, and the Dodge version (shown) was renamed the 600. Base price was dropped to $10,595.

1984 also brought a turbocharged engine option, available on both Dodge and Chrysler models. Dodge introduced the sporty 600 ES Turbo in '85.

Little was changed on the LeBaron for 1985, though prices were going up and now started at $11,889. Fender badges and hood vents indicate that this car is equipped with the turbo engine.

power door locks as standard equipment. A less lavishly equipped "Highline" series was offered as a lower-priced alternative, since the Premium was now up to $18,000.

Further refinements, as well as a new model, were added for 1989. Now included as standard equipment on all LeBaron convertibles were driver's side air bag and four-wheel disc brakes. A 2.5 turbo with twin balance shafts replaced the 2.2 turbo on the option sheet. New to the line was a sporty GTC model equipped with an intercooled 2.2 turbo engine (delivering 174-bhp vs. 150-bhp for the 2.5 turbo) linked to a Getrag 5-speed gearbox. Included too were heavy-duty 4-wheel disc brakes, quicker steering ratio, and 205/55 R16 unidirectional tires mounted on cast aluminum wheels.

Also debuting that year was the long-awaited TC, a two-seat convertible courtesy of a joint effort between Chrysler and Maserati. Built in Italy, it was offered in only one form: loaded. Standard was every power option imaginable, along with leather interior, four-wheel anti-lock disc brakes, and removable hardtop. Customers had a choice of either a 160-bhp intercooled 2.2 turbo with automatic, or 200-bhp, 16-valve turbocharged and intercooled 2.2 (developed by

Maserati) with Getrag 5-speed. The all-inclusive price was $30,000; there were no options.

Chrysler promised the TC would be a limited production car—and indeed it was. In fact, it was a little more limited than Chrysler had hoped. Despite the exotic hardware and Italian parentage, fewer than 3000 TCs found buyers that first year.

Competitors were fairly quick to chime in with convertibles of their own: Buick, as mentioned, for '82; Chevrolet and Ford for 1983; Pontiac and Cadillac (the latter to the ire of two lawyers with '76 Eldos—see previous chapter) for '84. Still, Chrysler gets the credit for reviving ragtops—ironic, as it had never been able to sell that many in the old days.

Chrysler and the others were only responding to the small but steady demand for American convertibles that had been met by aftermarket conversions in the factory ragtop's six-year absence. Given the economics of automaking in the Eighties and the fact that convertibles always sell in relatively low volume, it was only natural that they'd turn to the same companies for design and manufacturing assistance in building their own new models. Therefore, many of these

227

new-generation ragtops are not "factory built" the way the last Seventies models were (the LeBaron convertible is an exception), though you still buy them through your local dealer.

Ford likewise had success with its "new generation" Mustang convertible, introduced in 1983, averaging about 20,000 sales annually throughout the decade. Strangely, a convertible version of Mustang's clone, the Mercury Capri, was never offered. However, Capri failed to attract many buyers during this period (sales typically hovered at about 10 percent of its stablemate's figures), and the car itself was dropped after 1986.

To steal some of Chrysler's thunder, Ford first displayed its reborn ragtop as a 1982 prototype, but didn't start production until the facelifted '83 Mustangs were ready. Bowing in top-line GLX trim at around $11,000, this new flip-top Ford featured roll-down rear side windows, standard power top, and glass backlight. A new, 3.8 V-6 was standard, while the beloved 302-cubic-inch (5.0-liter) small-block V-8 was an option.

A rearranged '84 Mustang lineup presented three convertibles: base LX and two new GTs; V-8 and Turbo. The last, fussier to drive and costlier than the V-8 version, garnered few orders: a mere 600 or so that year (plus 2450 coupes). Exit Turbo GT.

All Mustangs got another nose job for '85, V-8 models another 25 horses. For '86, the 302 gained port fuel injection and a healthy 40 extra pounds-feet of torque. Come 1987 and Mustang was again facelifted, in line with Ford's "aero look." Strangely, the standard V-6 was dropped altogether and replaced by a normally-aspirated 2.3L four. The only optional engine by this time was the 302 V-8, so buyers had to choose between a 90-bhp weakling and a 225-bhp scorcher. The '88s and '89s were virtual reruns.

Prices, as would be expected, rose somewhat over the years, but were still well within reason. List price on the LX soft-top had gone up to just over $14,000 by '89, while the GT remained a real performance bargain at about $17,000 base. That extra three grand got you the 225-bhp V-8, five-speed manual transmission, firm suspension and limited-slip differential, along with special interior trim and "aero" bodywork. Those who felt the radical GT styling was a bit much could order the more conservative LX, specify the V-8 and GT chassis upgrades, and save a few bucks in the bargain.

The ragtop Riviera, introduced almost simultaneously with Highland Park's first soft-tops, was a logical step for the personal-luxury Buick. It was a good "image move" too, since Cadillac and Oldsmobile didn't immediately snip tops from their E-body cars, Eldorado and Toronado. Yet the Riviera

230

didn't sell so it didn't last long, 1985 being the last year it was offered (when production was only 400 units) after a total run of only about 4000 units. One reason was high price: $25,000 base, about $10,000 more than a comparable Riviera coupe.

Performance—or rather the lack of it—was another problem. Said *Collectible Automobile®* magazine: "Though Buick's 125-horsepower 4.1-liter V-6 was standard, it didn't move this 3800-pound car with much gusto, aggravated by the tall 'economy' gearing of GM's four-speed Turbo Hydramatic, the only transmission available. Fortunately, the extra-cost 140-bhp 307 V-8 (imported from Olds) was a no-charge convertible option, and we suspect most of the ragtops had it. Buick's 3.8 turbo V-6 was also theoretically available, but its accompanying T-Type equipment wasn't, so it's likely few, if any, convertibles were so endowed." As it was, the 4.1 gave you 0-60 mph in about 15 seconds and "economy" of 14 mpg.

At least the Riv was plush and quiet, thanks to a velour interior and extensive sound insulation. But *CA*'s editorial colleagues at CONSUMER GUIDE® complained about ride comfort: "All-independent suspension gives fine ride control on good roads, but wavy surfaces make the body rise and fall like a merry-go-round horse."

What really killed the open Riviera was GM's switch to even-smaller new E-body cars for 1986. Buyers truly rebelled at their high prices and styling that aped that of much cheaper GM models. It's doubtful that convertibles would have helped sales very much, as they would surely have cost more than the coupes. The official explanation for why the new Riv/Eldo/Toro had none was that a convertible conversion would have rendered the coupe's back seat unacceptably small. Fair enough, but GM had other plans, more on which will be discussed later.

Cadillac was rather slow to follow with a convertible version of its Riviera-cousin Eldorado. The reason was certainly not because it once promised to build no more convertibles but rather because of the Riviera's slow sales, which must have made Cadillac managers hesitate.

But they finally took the plunge for 1984 with a new ragtop Eldo, offered only in uplevel Biarritz trim. Like the Riv, it would vanish after '85. At $32,105 base, it was the most expensive U.S. production convertible ever built to that time, though price didn't kill it as much as the advent of that new E-body and the luxury market's continuing desertion to imports.

Cadillac later tried to stem the import tide—and polish up a quite tarnished image—with yet another, even costlier convertible: the Allante. Aimed at the big-bucks Mercedes 560SL (over $61,000 by 1988), Cadillac's first modern-day

production two-seater bowed with great fanfare for 1987 on a shortened (99.4-inch-wheelbase) Eldorado chassis with modified mechanicals. Power was initially supplied by the division's 4.1-liter transverse V-8 (as used in other front-drive Cadillacs through 1986) with multi-point (instead of single-point) fuel injection, roller valve lifters, high-flow cylinder heads and tuned intake manifold providing 170 bhp.

The Allante's tasteful but conservative styling was the work of Italy's renowned Pininfarina, which also built the body and shipped it to Detroit (by air!) from a factory near Turin. Aluminum hood and trunklid were fixed to a galvanized steel structure. Standard equipment was predictably complete, and included an SL-style lift-off hardtop to supplement the folding roof. The only option was a cellular telephone installed in a lockable between-seats bin and featuring the industry's first retractable AM/FM/telephone antenna.

Though a capable tourer and an entirely new breed of Cadillac, the Allante failed to make the hoped-for impression. Cadillac predicted 1987 model-year sales of 4000 units but got only 1651; for the first full production year, deliveries totaled just 2500 out of a planned 7000. The result: an embarrassing pile-up of unsold cars, rebates to clear it—and a further blow to Cadillac's prestige. *Automotive News* went so far as to call Allante the 1987 "Flop of the Year," though division chief John O. Grettenberger dismissed this and wide coverage of the car's slow start as "just the latest round of GM bashing."

Still, there were undeniable problems. As *AutoWeek*'s Chris Sawyer pointed out, the Allante was expensive for what it was—$54,000 at announcement, rising to $56,500 with the unchanged '88—yet it depreciated by a third the minute it left the showroom. The SL, by contrast, *appreciated* in value. Then too, Allante was plagued by the sort of niggling troubles not common in Mercedes: wind and water leaks around the top, miscellaneous squeaks and rattles, engine oil leaks, horns that didn't work, and heaters that worked too well.

Pontiac and Chevy introduced convertibles in 1983 based on the J-car platform—Cavalier and 2000 (later called the Sunbird), respectively—but volume was never close to that of Ford's or Chrysler's offerings.

After testing public reaction with a prototype, Chevy began selling the Cavalier convertible in limited numbers beginning late in the '83 model year, when only 627 were built. But the ragtop was more readily available and in a greater variety of color and trim combinations for '84. It sold as a sporty Type-10 (which formerly meant only a hatchback coupe) at just over $11,000 base. All '84 Cavaliers were handsomely facelifted with quad headlamps, cross-hatch grille, and body-color bumpers.

The subcompact Cavalier has long delivered excellent mileage and—since 1984—decent performance. But it's never been cheap for its class, and price must have caused a lot of buyers to think twice about signing for a convertible. Nevertheless, sales increased steadily through the decade, which is more than some convertible makers can claim. The '87s numbered 16,451, more than half of the 27,000-plus divisional total that made Chevy "USA-1" in convertibles for the first time since 1974.

Type-10 Cavaliers were renamed RS for 1986. Standard power remained the dull 2.0-liter overhead-valve four used since Cavalier's birth, but the convertible was optionally offered with the fine 2.8-liter Chevy V-6 from the new neo-muscle Z-24 hatchback. An extra-cost Getrag-designed five-speed manual transaxle was announced that year but didn't become available until '87, when "Generation II" improvements were applied to both engines.

A more substantial facelift considerably changed Cavalier's looks for '88. Even better, the RS convertible was made a Z-24, with standard V-6, "handling" suspension, all-season performance tires on aluminum wheels, and the sportiest premium interior. Only minor changes were made for '89, but by then, list price was over $16,500. That seemed a lot for a small car, even a rapid, roadable ragtop.

Symbolic of the convertible's resurgence was the mid-1986 debut of the first Corvette roadster in 11 years. Announced just in time to pace the Indy 500, it was based on the slightly smaller (96.2-inch-wheelbase) and lighter sixth-generation Corvette, introduced as a targa-top coupe in early 1983 for model year '84. It naturally shared most of the coupe's pluses: sleek styling, sophisticated all-independent suspension,

powerful 350 V-8, Bosch antilock braking system (from 1986), and more practical packaging. It also inherited most of the minuses: rocky ride, gimmicky electronic instruments, indifferent workmanship, and record prices—a little over $33,000 on introduction. Yet despite that, the reborn roadster (a misnomer; it remained a true convertible) sold quite well. Chevy moved 7264 for the balance of the '86 season and 10,625 for '87.

The sixth-generation 'Vette had been designed with a convertible in mind, and some of the necessary stiffening measures engineered for the roofless version showed up in the '87 coupe to answer complaints about body shake in earlier models. Specifically, K-braces were added to connect the front frame crossmember with the chassis siderails, door latches were strengthened, a crossmember applied behind the cockpit, and an X-brace tacked-on amidships. The convertible had slightly different rear-quarter contours and its own suspension tuning, which was midway between the coupe's stock setup and Z-51 handling option.

Recalling the original 1953 'Vette, the new roadster arrived with a manual top that folded beneath a rigid cover. The '86s were all considered Indy Pace Car Replicas and thus came with facsimile owner-applied decals (Detroit never seems to tire of this). Unlike previous commemorative Corvettes, however, the full range of factory body colors was available (the actual pacers were painted bright yellow).

Chevrolet brought back the Corvette convertible for 1986. Though the model pictured above is an '87, the two were virtually identical—save for an extra 10 horses (up to 240) on the '87.

Dodge lost its ragtop for 1987, but Chrysler's (below) received a complete redesign. By 1988, it was selling better than both previous models combined.

Pontiac facelifted its Sunbird with a sleeker front end for 1987. Shown below is the GT convertible, which got a more powerful (165-bhp) turbo engine.

Facelifted front and rear for 1988, the Cavalier came out much better looking. Also new for '88 was the sporty Z24 convertible (above), which based at $15,990.

Cadillac's Allante (above) remained unchanged for 1988. Production was running about 3000-3500 units per year, but sales weren't—many remained unsold.

Adoption of Tuned Port Injection (replacing the 1982-vintage dual throttle-body system) had lifted the venerable Chevy small-block from 205 to 230 SAE net horsepower by the time the roadster arrived. For 1987, roller valve lifters and other internal changes added 10 more, while raising torque to an impressive 345 pounds-feet (versus 290 the previous year). Result: 0-60-mph times of close to six seconds flat.

Model year '88 brought more tweaks that added another five horses for 245 total. Equally welcome were new-design wheels concealing larger and thicker all-disc brakes—which grew larger still with the newly optional 17-inch wheels shod with huge P275/40ZR-17 tires rated for speeds in excess of 149 mph. Talk about "wind in your hair" driving! Of course, few owners will ever approach that speed—or should—but we can all be grateful for the return of a great American tradition. *Vive la 'Vette!*

Corvette convertibles received some refinements for 1989, but the big news came in the form of a new coupe model—the

mighty ZR1. With a 32-valve, 385-bhp all-aluminum V-8 under the hood, this "King of the Hill" Corvette encroached on performance ground previously reserved only for European exotics. Two other innovations that debuted on the ZR1, however, did trickle down to the "regular" 'Vettes: a new six-speed manual gearbox and optional Selective Ride Control. The latter was available only with manual transmission and Z51 handling package, allowing three driver-selectable levels of shock damping—Touring, Sport, and Competition.

Other '89 developments included a faster steering ratio, redesigned seats (leather-covered sport seats with full-power lumbar adjustment and six-way positioning came with the Z51 handling package), and a more aggressive footprint (the previously optional 17-inch wheel/tire combination was made standard on all models). For convertibles, a detachable hardtop was offered as an option.

Chevy took more than four years to answer the open-air Mustang directly, but its new Camaro convertible, arriving in

Left: *After re-introducing the Camaro convertible for 1987 (the first since '69), Chevy saw little reason to change it for '88, seen here in IROC-Z form.*

Right: *Few changes were also made to the Corvette in '88, save for the addition of another 5 horsepower (to 245) and restyled wheels.*

January 1987, cheered dealers and enthusiasts alike. Another factory-approved conversion (by Automobile Specialty Company, a division of Detroit-based American Sunroof), it was offered in the same four guises as that year's closed Camaro: high-performance IROC-Z and Z-28, LT (Luxury Touring), and base V-6 Sport Coupe (was the last thus a "Sport Coupe convertible?"). Only 4000 were scheduled to be built that model year, all suitably reinforced to accommodate the soft top and engines that ran to the IROC's 5.7-liter, 220-bhp injected V-8. Base price was near $14,400, though a full-tilt IROC set you back another $3000 or more.

As it had with the T&C, 600ES Turbo and Riviera ragtops, *Collectible Automobile®* was quick to single out the convertible Camaro as a future collectible, the IROC in particular: "Even taking the rough ride and lousy gas mileage into consideration, the IROC-Z convertible is a blue-chip investment. Buy one now and enjoy it, take meticulous care of it, and it will return more than its original price somewhere down the road, and likely sooner than most people think...If history is a guide, demand will soon exceed supply...."

Possibly, though in today's unpredictable market, as Sam Goldwyn said, "all predictions are dangerous—especially about the future." Though the LT and Z-28 models were dropped for '88, the remaining IROC and base models were both cleanly styled and arguably the best-looking of the third-generation Camaros. For '89, the base model was given an RS tag along with swoopier bodywork that made it look like a pseudo IROC. The IROC also took a step forward,

offering 16-inch wheels shod with Z-rated tires and a 240-bhp version of the tried-and-true 5.7L V-8.

Pontiac began offering soft-top Sunbirds soon after the convertible Cavalier went on sale, but it wouldn't have Chevy's success. In 1986, for example, the Cav outsold the Bird 13 to three despite similar price tags (though possibly because of the greater number and higher volume of Chevy dealerships).

First cataloged in the uplevel LE series for 1984, the convertible was offered with the same three engines as other Sunbirds: Cavalier ohv four and normal and turbocharged versions of the new Opel-designed 1.8-liter overhead-cam four supplied to Pontiac (and Buick and Olds for their J-cars) by GM do Brasil. The LE became an SE for '86, when Pontiac added a new GT convertible with semi-hidden headlamps, rear spoiler, the turbo 1.8, and beefier Rally suspension. Both ohc engines grew to 2.0 liters as the main change for '87, while '88 brought a Cavalier-style "taillift" and an end to the soft-top SE—meaning that the turbo-engined GT was the only drop-top available. A new instrument panel arrived for '89 as the only significant change.

Oldsmobile, which prospered with convertibles so often, was the only GM division to ignore the '80s revival. While the "Gallant Men" had their own J-car clone (Firenza) as well as the Toronado (very similar to Buick's Riviera), Olds chose not to offer convertible versions of either—a shame really, particularly in the case of the Toronado.

Finally, a rather curious re-entry to the convertible ranks in the Eighties: good old never-say-die American Motors, by then in the hands of France's Renault—but only temporarily.

Buick built this interesting Regal convertible prototype in 1988, but odds are it will never see production.

As many expected, when the going got tough, Renault got going—out the door. Purchased by Chrysler in 1987, the AMC name was consigned to history, though some of its models lived on as offerings of the new Jeep-Eagle Division.

But before its 1987 takeover, AMC gave us a convertible version of the unmemorable front-drive Renault Alliance subcompact. Introduced for 1985, two years behind Alliance sedans and Encore hatchbacks, it actually put American Motors in fourth place for the first time since the Sixties— in convertible sales, that is. A factory-built job and AMC's first topless car since 1968, it was the cheapest convertible in the country: just over $10,000 without options. It was also remarkably light for a convertible: 2184 pounds, about 200 up on the two-door sedan. For $1000 more than the base L model, customers could have a DL, with better trim, reclining seats, five-speed overdrive manual transmission, extra insulation, and other amenities. It was no road-burner with the standard 1.4-liter four, but was more acceptable with that year's newly enlarged 1.7-liter option.

But despite the low price, it would have a short life. While it wasn't really all *that* bad, it competed in a market segment full of quicker, quieter, better-built cars. After two fairly strong years, sales plunged in 1985 owing to Japanese competition, a market swing to more expensive models, stable fuel prices, and Renault's poor U.S. reputation (something Alliance did little to improve). Convertibles suffered right along with other

models, dropping from 7143 to 1651 units for '86, hardly more than a trickle.

Still pushing water uphill, AMC came back for '87 with "pocket rocket" GTA models: a $9000 two-door sedan and a $13,000 convertible. A new 95-bhp 2.0-liter four delivered 0-60 in under 10 seconds, and an uprated suspension provided near sports-car cornering power (though claimed lateral acceleration was optimistic at 0.89G). But again, Alliance just didn't have enough of the "right stuff"—or perhaps too much of the wrong stuff. In any case, it was the first thing to go when Chrysler hung its sign on AMC's Kenosha, Wisconsin, factory (which it soon closed). Due primarily to its sportier nature and low sales volume, the GTA convertible actually stands a chance of becoming a collectors item someday—though a minor one to be sure.

And speaking of low volume cars, offerings from a couple of small, independent manufacturers deserve mention here. First, a convertible version of the venerable Avanti (which had been resurrected in 1965 as the Avanti II, and again in 1984 as simply the Avanti) appeared for 1987. Though the exterior looked much as it had when the car first hit the automotive scene 24 years earlier, the interior and mechanicals had been duly updated to more current standards. Power was provided by a 305-cid Chevy V-8 producing 185-bhp or 205-bhp optionally. Introductory price for the hand-crafted, fiberglass-bodied convertible was about

To celebrate the Mustang's 25th Anniversary, a special limited-edition 1989 convertible was offered in "deep emerald-jewel green-metallic clearcoat" with white top and leather interior.

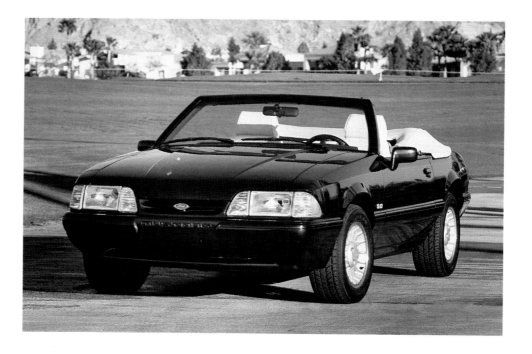

A specially-prepared Oldsmobile Cutlass Supreme convertible paced the Indy 500 in 1988—a vision of things to come? Note '49 Olds Pace Car in background.

$40,000, a figure that jumped considerably by decade-end. Production figures are unavailable for 1987 (the year assembly was moved from South Bend, Indiana, to Youngstown, Ohio), but 1988 saw 125 convertibles come down the line, followed by 151 in 1989. For 1990, the company ceased (at least temporarily) production of both the coupe and convertible in order to concentrate on its new 4-door sedan.

Secondly, let us not forget Excalibur. Fashioned after the 1928 Mercedes SSK two-seat roadster, the first prototype appeared in 1964 astride a Studebaker Lark convertible chassis. Power was supplied by a supercharged, 290-bhp, 289-cid Studebaker V-8, but the production cars that followed carried a 327-cid Corvette engine. These first examples were priced at $7250—about $3000 more than a Corvette— yet were hand-built cars with ample power and fine road manners. Though early versions were somewhat spartan, by 1969 both two- and four-seat models were offered that came fully equipped with automatic transmission, air conditioning, tilt steering wheel, chrome-plated wire wheels, Positraction, twin side-mounted spare tires, and self-leveling rear shocks—yet still carried side curtains. True convertibles (with roll-up windows) didn't appear until 1980, and while the two models continued to be called "Roadster" and "Phaeton," they were more accurately "convertible coupes," at least by definition. Chevy power was retained throughout the years— small blocks (327/350) until 1972, big block 454s through

'78, then back to small blocks (350/305) due to government regulations. By 1980, prices had escalated to almost $38,000; by the end of the decade, they were up to about $72,000. The number built varied (sometimes greatly) from year to year: Through the early Seventies, production usually hovered around 75 units annually, after which it increased somewhat, but rarely exceeded 300 as a combined total. The fledgling company struggled on through the '80s, but by 1990 had filed for chapter 11.

While some of the convertibles introduced in the '80s would not live to see the end of the decade, the revival as a whole must be considered a resounding success. Much of this can be attributed to the advent of outside specialty firms capable of performing the conversions, thereby freeing the manufacturers from prohibitive investments in time, money, and assembly space. Actually, this was not so much a new idea as it was an example of history repeating itself. Back in the early days of the convertible, many manufacturers approached independent coach builders to supply custom bodies for what promised to be low-production cars—and often for the same reason.

At the close of the decade, there were no fewer than eight convertibles being offered by the Big Three—most through GM. Though still a very small percentage of total industry volume, production exceeded 150,000 units for 1989, enough to ensure the breed's survival into the Nineties.

After experiencing phenomenal success with its early ragtops, Chrysler went upmarket in 1989 with the $30,000 Maserati-built TC. Supply exceeded demand.

1990–91

T H E   T R E N D
C O N T I N U E S . . .

1991 Chevrolet Corvette

*Considering their cost, it's somewhat amazing that this new crop of drop-tops sells as well as it does. Today, convertible production is at a level not seen since the late Sixties. But then, they **are** convertibles, and since 1927, that's one of the nicest things a car can be.*

Some may have questioned whether the ragtop's revival might result in only temporary popularity—an automotive "flash-in-the-pan"—with sales declining as soon as the novelty wore off. For those not satisfied that the convertible's burgeoning popularity through the end of the Eighties was a reliable indication, the Nineties will no doubt provide their answer.

All of the convertibles available from the "Big Three" in 1989 carried over into the Nineties with little change—except one. Despite a strong third-place showing on the sales charts in recent years, the Chevy Cavalier convertible was dropped at the end of 1989. While it was due to be replaced by a new Beretta ragtop, conversion problems delayed—and finally denied—the Beretta's arrival. This left Chevrolet dealers with just the Corvette and two Camaro convertibles for 1990, three cars with a combined volume only slightly higher than that of the lone Cavalier model.

Otherwise, Chevy changed little for 1990. A 3.1 V-6 replaced the 2.8 as the standard engine for Camaro RS, while the Corvette received a new, "half moon" instrument panel with a combination of analog and digital gauges. All Camaros and Corvettes gained driver's side airbags.

Likewise, 1991 models saw only minor updates. Chevrolet dropped sponsorship of the International Race of Champions (from which IROCs got their name), so it was no longer authorized to use that moniker. This prompted the reappearance of the Z28 logo on the top-line Camaro after a three-year absence. Otherwise, the sporty 2+2 was basically unchanged. Corvettes received no major mechanical alterations, but did get rectangular taillamps (*à la* ZR-1), "gills" added behind the front wheel wells, and a smoother front facia.

Above: *Buick introduced a ragtop version of its limited-production Reatta in the spring of 1990. About 2200 were built for the model year at $35,000.*

Opposite: *A production version (prototype in foreground) of the Chevy Beretta ragtop that paced the 1990 Indy 500 (background) was planned, but never offered.*

Below: *Interior view of 1990 Buick Reatta ragtop shows leather-lined cockpit, airbag-equipped steering wheel, and vacuum-fluorescent display instruments.*

Pontiac made similarly minor alterations to the Sunbird convertible for 1990. Available only in a GT version since '88, it was now based on the lower-line LE in an effort to boost sales by cutting prices. Starting at under $14,000, it was over $2000 less than the '89. Base engine was the 96-bhp normally-aspirated 2.0; the turbo version with 165-bhp was available as a package option. The most notable change for '91 was the substitution of a 3.1L V-6 for the turbo four on the options list.

Cadillac's slow-selling Allante gained two noteworthy features for 1990: a driver's side airbag and traction control. The latter was the first use of such a device in a front-wheel-drive car, employing both brake application and power cut-off to minimize wheel spin under slippery conditions. Furthermore, Cadillac added a less expensive, "de-contented" version of the car, *sans* bolt-on hardtop and with analog (instead of digital) instrumentation. The Allante soldiered on with only minor changes for '91.

Buick ventured back into the convertible market with a $35,000, drop-top version of its hand-built, two-passenger Reatta—a bold move considering the cool reception given to the similar Chrysler TC, Cadillac Allante, and the ill-fated '80s Riviera ragtops. Launched in mid-'90, it came fully equipped with only a CD player and 16-way power driver's seat as options. Like the coupe, which was introduced in 1988, it was conceived not as a sports car, but as a personal, two-place luxury car more in keeping with Buick's traditional clientele. Despite rather compact dimensions (wheelbase was only 98.5 inches), neither Reatta was particularly light; 3350 lbs for the coupe, 3550 for the convertible. Power for both versions came from the corporate 165-bhp "3800" V-6, which provided adequate, though not outstanding, acceleration.

Above: *1990 Mustang GT boasted a 225-bhp, 302-cid V-8 and gained a driver's airbag. Base price was about $18,800 – a performance bargain.* Right: *Though sold by Geo dealers, the Metro ragtop was built entirely in Japan.*

Performance improved slightly in 1991, however, when "tuned port injection" was added to the 3800 (bringing with it five more horsepower), which drove through a new, electronically-controlled 4-speed automatic and lower axle ratio.

For the first time since 1975, Oldsmobile entered the convertible fray by introducing a ragtop rendition of its front-wheel-drive Cutlass Supreme. Production didn't begin until late in the 1990 model year, and only 450 were built (at $21,000 each) before the changeover to '91s—not that there was much difference. The only engine/transmission combination offered for '90 and '91 was a 3.1L V-6 pumping out 140-bhp through a 4-speed automatic. The convertible was no lightweight (3600 lbs., vs. 3200 for the 2-door coupe on which it was based), so performance was "gentlemanly," at best. Sadly, a 3.4L, dohc, 200-bhp V-6 added to the Cutlass

Supreme's option list for 1991 was not offered in the convertible.

Unique to the Olds ragtop was a "targa bar," which was originally the car's B-pillar. (Chevy's stillborn Beretta carried a similar design.) Though claimed to have been preserved to add strength to the structure (which it probably did, to some extent), it also carried the door handles and the shoulder belt anchors—items that would have been costly to reposition. The Cutlass convertible came standard with air conditioning, a power-operated top, full-width back seat, fully finished headliner, glass backlight, and a power window system that could lower all four windows at once. While well-equipped, it was not loaded; optional were ABS, upgraded radios, rear-window defogger, full instrumentation, leather upholstery, and a sports package.

Chrysler carried its LeBaron convertible—the best-selling

ragtop in the land—into the '90s with a number of meaningful changes. There were now four models: Highline, Premium, Highline GT, and Premium GTC. Instrument panels on all were given a "half moon" shell with round, analog gauges. Two new engines and transmissions were offered: the Mitsubishi-built 3.0L V-6 that could be teamed with an electronically-controlled 4-speed automatic; and an intercooled 2.2 with variable-nozzle turbocharger (VNT) producing 174-bhp that could be ordered with a heavy-duty 5-speed manual on the GTC. Also new was an optional Electronic Vehicle Information Center, security alarm, and for the GTC, variable suspension. Strangely, the much-touted VNT 2.2 disappeared after one year, replaced by a beefed-up 2.5 turbo with 152-bhp. Otherwise, there were few changes for 1991.

The ill-begotten two-seat TC also got some changes at the start of the decade, but they were relatively minor. An airbag was incorporated into a wood-rimmed steering wheel, and the Mitsubishi 3.0L V-6 replaced the intercooled eight-valve turbo when the automatic transmission was ordered. Sales were still dismal; of the 7300 that were produced in total, 2924 were sold during the '89 model year, 3997 in '90. The remainder were re-serialed as '91s.

The TC notwithstanding, Chrysler felt the demand for convertibles was strong enough to allow for the introduction of a third ragtop for 1991. This one, however, went downmarket; based on the Dodge Shadow, it started at about $13,000. As such, it was the lowest-priced convertible built in America. To meet this goal, however, certain "niceties" were made optional or left off altogether. One such item was a power top; the Shadow didn't even offer it as an option.

One interesting note. Though we've been discussing only cars here, Chrysler made waves in 1990 by following a West Coast trend and introducing a convertible pickup truck based on the mid-sized Dakota. Alas, the wave quickly calmed to a

Left: *For 1990, Pontiac offered its Sunbird convertible only in low-line LE guise. The example pictured is equipped with the 165-bhp turbocharged engine.*

Below: *Though looking far different than its Indy-pacing predecessor, Oldsmobile finally introduced a Cutlass convertible in late 1990, priced at $20,995.*

For 1991, Chevrolet continued the Camaro convertible with two models: the RS (shown at right) and the reincarnated Z28. RS prices started at $17,960.

ripple, and the drop-top Dakota soon joined the TC in the "you can't win 'em all" category.

Unlike GM and Chrysler, Ford stuck with a single offering since joining the ragtop market back in 1983. And despite its age, the Mustang continues to do very well, thank you, consistently nailing down the number two spot in convertible sales. Furthermore, it has accomplished this feat with no more than minor year-to-year updates. In fact, there's little to report about the newer models: Airbags were added to all Mustangs in 1990, and '91 brought a twin-plug head to the 2.3L four, raising output from 88- to 105-bhp.

We've barely made mention in these pages of convertibles offered by foreign manufacturers, since they are beyond the scope of this book. However, the Nineties have brought changes to the marketplace that make it increasingly difficult to label a vehicle as import or domestic. First of all, several foreign manufacturers are now building vehicles in this country. Volkswagen started the trend in the late Seventies

(though it has since pulled out), with a number of the major Japanese companies following suit. Secondly, there are the joint ventures: Ford's Probe is being made at a Mazda plant in Michigan; the Geo Prism is assembled alongside the similar Toyota Corolla in California; and the Diamond-Star facility in Illinois produces cars for both its parent companies, Chrysler and Mitsubishi. Furthermore, all of the Big Three have sold vehicles bearing their own brands that were actually designed and built overseas. The point is that the distinction between "import" and "domestic" is becoming ever more blurred.

While we have omitted those vehicles built and/or sold by foreign companies, sharp readers may question the inclusion of the Cadillac Allante and Chrysler TC by Maserati (both of which have their bodies built in Italy). These two have been discussed because they carry domestic drivetrains and are sold primarily in this country; vehicles like the '91 Geo Metro convertible (by Suzuki of Japan) and Mercury Capri (made

Above: *Z28 replaced the former IROC-Z as the top-performance Camaro after Chevy discontinued sponsorship of the IROC racing series. Price of entry: $20,815.*

For 1991, Chrysler offered three LeBaron convertibles, with base prices ranging from $15,925 to $19,175. This GTC (above) started at $18,100.

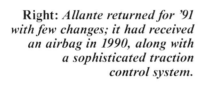

Left: *Dodge Shadow was a new convertible entry for 1991, with base prices starting at $13,000. The sporty ES model shown was about $1000 more.*

Right: *Allante returned for '91 with few changes; it had received an airbag in 1990, along with a sophisticated traction control system.*

Left: *Corvette's convertible got a few styling revisions for 1991, most notably rectangular taillights, a smoother front end, and different wheels.*

Above: *Pontiac Sunbird's turbo engine was dropped for 1991 and replaced with a 3.1L V-6.* **Below, left:** *Of the 7300 Chrysler TCs built in total, only about 7000 had been sold at the end of the 1990 model year. The remainder were reserialed as '91s.* **Below, right:** *1991 Mustang GT got new wheels, but little else.*

in Australia using Mazda powertrains) are built entirely overseas and widely distributed in their home markets as well as in the U.S.

There's one last point about the revival of the convertible that we can't help but make. It has to do with prices—or more precisely, *relative* prices. For instance, to purchase a Chrysler LeBaron convertible in 1982, one had to shell out nearly $14,000—almost $5600 more than its coupe counterpart, or a premium of about 66 percent. The '83 Mustang was similar: $12,467 for the base convertible vs. $7557 for the base coupe; a 65-percent surcharge. The *percentage* figures have come down slightly in recent years, but only because car prices in general have risen while conversion costs have remained about the same. Nevertheless, compare this to 25 years ago: a Mustang coupe went for $2416; a convertible, $2653. The difference? $237, or less than 10 percent. Over at Chevy, it was the same story. An Impala coupe based at $2789 while the ragtop was $3041; a difference of $252, or just over nine percent. Sigh.

Considering current price differentials, it's somewhat amazing that this new crop of drop-tops sells as well as it does. Today, convertible production is at a level not seen since the late Sixties. But then, they *are* convertibles, and since 1927, that's one of the nicest things a car can be.

At this point, at least, the convertible's future appears secure. More and more variations are showing up on the market every year, giving aficionados an ever-widening selection of models from which to choose. And as long as this trend continues, the essence of romance—automotive and otherwise—will surely be alive and well in America.

Since only 450 of the 1990 Cutlass convertibles were built before the new model changeover, the '91 (above) saw few changes.

The Australian-built 1991 Capri finally made it to Mercury showrooms in mid-1990. The turbocharged XR2 version (above) was priced at $15,522.

PRODUCTION FIGURES

1931 Chevy Independence

It is fascinating to trace the ups and downs of convertible production, but determining exact counts is quite difficult. Industry figures are commonly nebulous, or estimated, or sometimes (as for 1927-30 and 1936-40) nonexistent. Moreover, sources that do exist may disagree, forcing the researcher to either accept one source or strike an average.

Most estimates herein were arrived at by dividing the total figure for each make (including estimates where figures are not available), by model year production. While this yields a decent approximation, it cannot be exact because some manufacturers quoted calendar year rather than model year output. (The high percentage in 1942 is an anomaly, but this war-abbreviated year should never be used as a yardstick anyway.)

Where we are blessed with several sources, the best industry records have been accepted: *Polk's* over *Ward's* or *Automotive News,* for example. Between 1947 and 1976, serious attention was paid to the statistics published by R. Perry Zavitz in the Spring 1976 (No. 15) issue of *The Milestone Car,* on the grounds that his research was more recent and more painstaking than the rest.

Calendar Year Production

Cal. Year	Total Number Convertibles	Percent of Total Prod.
1927	2,600*	0.01
1928	10,000*	0.02
1929	25,000*	0.06
1930	40,000*	1.5
1931	85,314	4.2
1932	42,103	3.6
1933	22,823	1.4
1934	38,905	1.7
1935	41,917	1.2
1936	40,000*	1.1
1937	35,000*	0.9
1938	27,000*	1.4
1939	37,000*	1.3
1940	55,000*	1.5
1941	98,335	2.7
1942	20,000*	9.4
1946	45,000*	2.1
1947	173,863	4.9
1948	196,597	5.0
1949	215,635	4.2
1950	208,090	3.1
1951	143,388	2.7
1952	100,116	2.3
1953	154,500*	2.5
1954	131,500*	2.7
1955	212,000*	3.0
1956	210,000*	3.4
1957	266,000*	4.3
1958	193,717	4.6
1959	257,200*	4.6
1960	313,700*	4.7
1961	271,600*	4.9
1962	437,659	6.3
1963	489,824	6.4
1964	498,494	6.3
1965	509,415	5.5
1966	394,679	4.6
1967	306,078	4.1
1968	276,731	3.1
1969	201,997	2.5
1970	91,863	1.4
1971	87,725	1.0
1972	61,655	0.7
1973	50,837	0.5
1974	27,955	0.5
1975	8,950	0.1
1976	14,000	0.2
1977	0	0.0
1978	0	0.0
1979	0	0.0
1980	0	0.0
1981	36	0.0005
1982	9,900*	0.2
1983	40,600*	0.7
1984	57,525*	0.7
1985	63,275*	0.8
1986	76,520*	1.0
1987	77,300*	1.0
1988	111,100*	1.5
1989	123,100*	1.8

*estimate

Leading Producers
by Model Year

1927	1928	1929		1957	1958	1959
Buick	Buick	Ford		Ford	Chevrolet	Chevrolet
Chrysler	Chrysler	Dodge		Chevrolet	Ford	Ford
Cadillac	Packard	Buick		Olds	Olds	Pontiac
				Buick	Pontiac	Buick
				Pontiac	Buick	Olds

1930	1931	1932		1960	1961	1962
Ford	Chevrolet	Chevrolet		Chevrolet	Chevrolet	Chevrolet
Olds	Ford	Plymouth		Ford	Ford	Ford
Dodge	Olds	Ford		Pontiac	Pontiac	Pontiac
				Buick	Buick	Buick
				Olds	Cadillac	Olds

1933	1934	1935		1963	1964	1965
Ford	Ford	Ford		Chevrolet	Chevrolet	Ford
Plymouth	Plymouth	Olds		Ford	Ford	Chevrolet
Chevrolet	Chevrolet	Plymouth		Pontiac	Pontiac	Pontiac
				Buick	Buick	Buick
				Olds	Olds	Olds

1936	1937	1938		1966	1967	1968
Ford	Ford	Ford		Ford	Chevrolet	Chevrolet
Buick	Buick	Buick		Chevrolet	Ford	Pontiac
Chevrolet	Plymouth	Chevrolet		Pontiac	Pontiac	Ford
				Buick	Buick	Buick
				Olds	Olds	Olds

1939	1940	1941		1969	1970	1971
Ford	Chevrolet	Buick		Chevrolet	Chevrolet	Chevrolet
Plymouth	Ford	Chevrolet		Pontiac	Olds	Olds
Buick	Buick	Ford		Ford	Ford	Ford
Chevrolet	Plymouth	Plymouth		Olds	Buick	Buick
				Buick	Pontiac	Pontiac

1942	1946	1947		1972	1973	1974
Buick	Ford	Buick		Chevrolet	Chevrolet	Chevrolet
Ford	Buick	Chevrolet		Olds	Ford	Cadillac
Plymouth	Mercury	Ford		Ford	Cadillac	Olds
Dodge	Chevrolet	Olds		Buick	Olds	Buick
				Pontiac	Buick	Pontiac

1948	1949	1950		1975	1982	1983
Buick	Ford	Ford		Olds	Dodge	Ford
Chevrolet	Chevrolet	Chevrolet		Chevrolet	Chrysler	Chrysler
Olds	Buick	Pontiac		Cadillac	Buick	Dodge
Pontiac	Olds	Buick		Buick	—	Buick
Studebaker	Mercury	Olds		Pontiac	—	Chevrolet

1951	1952	1953		1984	1985	1986
Ford	Ford	Ford		Ford	Chrysler	Ford
Chevrolet	Chevrolet	Chevrolet		Chrysler	Dodge	Chrysler
Buick	Buick	Olds		Dodge	Ford	Dodge
Plymouth	Olds	Buick		Chevrolet	AMC	Chevrolet
Pontiac	Pontiac	Pontiac		Pontiac	Chevrolet	Pontiac

1954	1955	1956		1987	1988	1989	1990
Ford	Ford	Ford		Ford	Chrysler	Chrysler	Chrysler
Chevrolet	Chevrolet	Chevrolet		Chevrolet	Ford	Ford	Ford
Buick	Buick	Buick		Chrysler	Chevrolet	Chevrolet	Pontiac
Olds	Pontiac	Olds		Pontiac	Pontiac	Cadillac	Chevrolet
Pontiac	Olds	Pontiac		AMC	Cadillac	Pontiac	Cadillac

Convertible Production by Make

It is not possible to obtain model year production figures for each make building convertibles. At various times, some makes record calendar year figures, sales or registration totals, but not model year production—the figure which most enthusiasts care most about.

Estimates based on known convertible percentages of overall model year output are therefore indicated with an asterisk (*), while calendar year figures are indicated with two asterisks (**).

In order to show when convertibles were being produced by each maker, two other designations have been used: "NA" (figures of any kind not available) and "0" (the make was in production, but did not produce convertibles).

Model Year	1927	1928	1929	1930	1931	1932	1933	1934	1935	1936	1937
Auburn-C-D		NA	NA	NA	NA	NA	NA	NA	NA	NA	
Buick	2,373	6,555	2,112	0	1,540	1,696	899	1,660	1,660	3,646	6,767
Cadillac	NA	NA	NA	NA	NA	NA	NA	NA	NA	NA	NA
Chevrolet					28,711	NA	4,276	3,276	0	3,629	1,724
Chrysler	200*	1,778	1,500*	1,900*	2,700*	1,600*	2,296	1,150	101	1,252	2.085
De Soto				700*	1,000*	1,000*	544	0	226	465	1,418
Dodge			2,400*	2,000*	750*	500*	1,658	1,239	950	2,275	1,818
Essex						NA	NA				
Ford			16,421**	26,868**	16,665**	8,205	8,800*	15,500*	21,536	19,669	14,562
Franklin		NA	NA	NA	NA	NA	NA	NA			
Graham		NA	NA	NA	0	NA	NA	NA	NA	NA	NA
Hudson						NA	NA	NA	NA	NA	NA
Hupp			NA	NA	NA	NA	NA	NA	0	0	0
La Salle		NA	NA	NA	NA	NA	NA	NA	NA	NA	NA
Lincoln	20*	NA	NA	200*	300*	50*	200*	275*	100*	100*	50*
Nash		NA	NA								
Oldsmobile				3,006	3,501	1,117	584	915	2,508	3,067	2,347
Packard		NA	NA	NA	NA	NA	NA	NA	NA	NA	NA
Plymouth				550*	725*	8,326	6,630	4,482	2,308	3,297	3,110
Pontiac		NA	NA	NA	NA	NA	NA	NA	NA	NA	NA
Studebacker		NA	NA	NA	NA	NA	NA	NA	0	0	0
Terraplane								NA	NA	NA	NA

Model Year	1938	1939	1940	1941	1942	1946	1947	1948	1949
Buick	4,895	5,659	9,729	19,403	4,788	8,574	40,371	30,520	30,354
Cadillac	396	564	354	3,500	308	1,342	6,755	5,450	8,000
Chevrolet	2,787	0	11,820	15,296	1,182	4,508	28,443	20,471	32,392
Chrysler	959	0	1,900*	5,727	975	500*	5,766**	6,215**	4,700**
De Soto	519	0	1,085	2,937	568	300*	2,969**	3,257*	3,500**
Dodge	833	0	2,100	3,554	1,185	500*	3,823**	3,826**	2,500**
Ford	7,445	13,983	10,000*	12,800*	3,000*	17,568	24,409	12,061	51,133
Frazer									70*
Graham	0	0	0	0					
Hudson	NA	NA	NA	1,052**	NA	1,175*	1,823**	1,188**	3,119**
Hupp	0	0	0	0					
Kaiser									54*
La Salle	1,120	1,241	1,224						
Lincoln	1,182	946	775*	1,125	327	1,000*	1,616**	2,516**	743**

*estimate   **calendar year

Model Year	1938	1939	1940	1941	1942	1946	1947	1948	1949
Mercury		NA	NA	4,900	1,230	6,044	10,221	7,586	16,765
Nash	NA	NA	NA	NA	0	0	0	999	0
Oldsmobile	1,659	2,186	2,757	5,297	1,000*	2,283	10,468	16,806	23,374
Packard	NA	NA	NA	NA	NA	0	0	8,868	2,127
Plymouth	1,900	6,363	6,986	10,545	2,806	NA	5,089**	6,048**	16,300**
Pontiac	NA	NA	NA	5,981**	NA	NA	10,020**	15,937**	14,795**
Studebaker	NA	NA		0	0	0	3,754	17,978	8,737

*estimate   **calendar year

Model Year	1950	1951	1952	1953	1954	1955	1956	1957	1958	1959
Buick	15,223	13,126	9,906	15,991	16,409	23,863	21,676	19,018	10,110	21,429
Cadillac	6,986	6,117	6,400	8,899	8,460	12,100	10,450	10,800	8,640	12,450
Chevrolet	32,810	20,172	11,975	29,664	19,383	41,292	44,735	53,901	65,157	82,435
Chrysler	3,100	4,700*	2,400*	2,200	1,225	2,341	1,932	1,533	859	1,387
De Soto	2,900	2,600*	2,200*	1,700	1,025	1,400	2,100*	2,748	1,775	1,200*
Dodge	4,703	4,250*	2,300*	4,100	2,050	3,302	3,339	NA	NA	NA
Edsel									2,806	1,343
Ford	50,299	40,934	22,534	40,861	36,685	66,121	73,778	119,882	51,876	69,044
Franklin										
Frazer	R/S	128*								
Hudson	3,322	1,651	636	NA	NA	0	0	0		
Imperial						1	0	1,167	675	555
Kaiser	R/S	0	0	0	0	0				
Lincoln	536	857	1,191	2,372	1,951	1,487	2,447	3,676	3,048	2,195
Mercury	8,341	6,759	5,261	8,463	7,293	10,668	10,073	10,546	3,989	5,680
Nash	9,330	NA	NA	NA	NA	0	0	0		
Oldsmobile	14,025	8,322	8,706	16,289	13,252	18,156	18,142	21,829	13,860	20,900
Packard	677	2,001	963	2,268	1,263	500	276	0	0	
Plymouth	12,697	9,500*	6,150*	6,301	6,900	8,473	6,735	9,866	9,941	11,053
Pontiac	19,696	9,470	8,502	13,500	12,374**	19,762	13,510	12,789	10,455	25,941
Rambler								0	0	0
Studebaker	13,229	8,512	3,290	0	0	0	0	0	0	0

R/S = Reserialed from previous year.

Model Year	1960	1961	1962	1963	1964	1965	1966	1967	1968	1969
Buick	25,570	23,062	37,615	40,637	38,249	38,023	29,826	25,213	27,447	22,616
Cadillac	15,285	16,950	18,250	19,425	19,770	21,325	21,450	18,202	18,025	16,445
Chevrolet	90,164	73,563	127,986	155,094	150,025	134,367	100,000*	84,395	75,266	58,044
Chrysler	2,271	3,048	4,022	5,489	4,202	5,050	5,585	4,485	5,008	4,102
De Soto	0	0								
Dodge	8,817	4,361	6,024	16,748	NA	NA	NA	NA	NA	NA
Edsel	76									

*estimate   **calendar year

Model Year	1960	1961	1962	1963	1964	1965	1966	1967	1968	1969
Ford	56,622	55,130	64,286	71,185	82,156	157,085	122,247	78,525	52,345	33,874
Imperial	618	429	554	922	633	514	577	474	0	
Lincoln	2,044	2,857	3,212	3,138	3,328	3,356	3,180	2,276	0	0
Mercury	7,587	7,053	6,804	18,273	16,524	13,803	13,879	6,357	5,875	13,436
Oldsmobile	25,385	15,477	36,607	33,368	33,181	31,478	27,000*	25,000*	25,973	27,611
Plymouth	7,080	6,948	5,865	25,333	22,523	20,924	15,512	15,486	14,132	11,933
Pontiac	34,234	30,643	59,094	62,677	72,899	72,951	62,571	63,736	53,975	38,014
Rambler	0	NA	13,497	NA	8,904	12,334	NA	1,200	0	0
Studebaker	8,571	1,981	2,681	1,015	703	0	0			

*estimate **calendar year

Model Year	1970	1971	1972	1973	1974	1975	1976	1977	1978	1979
AMC	0	0	0	0	0	0	0	0	0	0
Buick	16,146	8,912	8,893	5,739	3,627	5,300	0	0	0	0
Cadillac	15,172	6,800	7,975	9,315	7,600	8,950	14,000	0	0	0
Chevrolet	25,000*	16,786	17,817	13,432	10,144	12,978	0	0	0	0
Chrysler	2,201	0	0	0	0	0	0	0	0	0
Dodge	6,305	2,165	0	0	0	0	0	0	0	0
Ford	17,960	13,484	10,635	11,853	0	0	0	0	0	0
Imperial	0	0	0	0	0	0				
Lincoln	0	0	0	0	0	0	0	0	0	0
Mercury	6,113	3,440	3,169	4,449	0	0	0	0	0	0
Oldsmobile	20,543	14,442	15,471	7,088	3,716	21,038	0	0	0	0
Plymouth	6,262	1,388	0	0	0	0	0	0	0	0
Pontiac	15,676	8,368	8,050	4,447	3,000	4,519	0	0	0	0

Model Year	1980	1981	1982	1983	1984	1985	1986	1987	1988	1989	1990
AMC	0	0	0	0	0	7,143	1,651	1,991			
Avanti	0	0	0	0	0	0	0	NA	125	151	0
Buick	0	0	1,248	1,750	500	400	0	0	0	0	2,132
Cadillac	0	0	0	0	3,300	2,300	0	3,363	3,502	3,066	3,018
Chevrolet	0	0	0	627	5,486	4,108	20,313	27,076	21,772	27,778	8,902
Chrysler	0	0	3,045	9,891	16,208	20,191	19,684	8,025	41,263	52,338	45,975
Dodge	0	0	5,541	4,888	10,960	17,713	16,437	0	0	0	0
Excalibur	0	36	60	NA	NA	NA	NA	NA	NA	NA	NA
Ford	0	0	0	23,438	17,600	15,110	22,946	21,447	35,500	42,244	26,958
Imperial		0	0	0							
Lincoln	0	0	0	0	0	0	0	0	0	0	0
Mercury	0	0	0	0	0	0	0	0	0	0	0
Oldsmobile	0	0	0	0	0	0	0	0	0	0	450
Plymouth	0	0	0	0	0	0	0	0	0	0	0
Pontiac	0	0	0	0	3,447	3,830	2,752	3,452	3,542	2,863	12,812

*estimate **calendar year

INDEX